**Instructor's Manual
with Test Questions**

LEADERSHIP
IN
ORGANIZATIONS

Instructor's Manual with Test Questions

LEADERSHIP IN ORGANIZATIONS

Third Edition

GARY YUKL

State University of New York at Albany

Prentice Hall, Englewood Cliffs, NJ 07632

© 1994 by Prentice-Hall, Inc.
A Paramount Communications Company
Englewood Cliffs, N.J. 07632

10   9   8   7   6   5   4   3   2   1

ISBN 0-13-530882-8
Printed in the United States of America

Contents

Role Plays and Other Exercises

Test Bank

Preface

This manual is designed to facilitate learning of material in the third edition of *Leadership in Organizations*. The manual contains general guidelines for using cases and specific instructions for each of the 29 cases in the book. Answers to the case questions are also included.

The manual also contains some role plays and other types of experiential exercises to help students learn the skills important for effective leadership. There are general guidelines for using role plays and specific instructions for each role play and supplementary exercise. To use the role plays and exercises it is necessary to copy the appropriate pages in this manual and distribute them to students.

The approximate amount of class time required for each case and exercise is indicated in the instructions. Of course, the actual time will vary somewhat depending on how a case or exercise is used.

Finally, the manual contains a test bank with multiple choice items that measure specific knowledge of leadership concepts, theories, research findings, and effective behaviors.

The manual is organized by type of activity, not by book chapter. The first section of the manual deals with cases, the second section deals with exercises, and the third section deals with exams. In the Table of Contents, the relevant chapter for each case or exercise is noted in parentheses.

This edition of the leadership book is the first to have cases and exercises to facilitate learning and make the material more interesting for students. I welcome feedback from professors who use the cases and exercises to make this aspect of the book even stronger in future editions. Let me know what worked well, what problems were discovered, and what improvements are needed. If you discover other cases and exercises that are especially relevant and effective for teaching leadership skills, please let me know about them also.

Cases

General Guidelines for Using Cases

The cases provide concrete examples of the abstract conceptions and principles discussed in the book. Most of the cases provide a detailed description of the actions of a particular manager. The case questions usually ask students to identify examples of appropriate and inappropriate behavior by the manager. In cases where the manager has been ineffective, students are also asked to consider what should have been done by the manager. Finally, students are sometimes asked to recommend what the manager should do next.

For the longer and more complex cases, it is usually best to have students analyze the case alone as homework and come to class prepared to discuss it. The shorter and less complex cases can be read and analyzed right in class, but the analysis is usually better when done as homework prior to class. After the case is analyzed individually by students, an important choice is whether to discuss the case in the entire class or to form small discussion groups that will report back to the class on their findings and recommendations. Small groups allow more opportunity for active participation by students in the discussion, but more time is usually required for this option. A mix of the two approaches provides nice variety in the class.

The following guidelines will facilitate learning from the cases used in the book. Some of the guidelines assume the use of small groups to analyze a case following individual preparation as prework.

1. When assigning cases to students, explain the purpose of the case and how it will be used. Tell students what type of analysis they are expected to prepare for class.

2. The focus of the initial analysis should be to understand the leadership dilemmas in the case and what the case says about effective leadership, not to find solutions for specific problems. In making this analysis, students should try to use the concepts and theories discussed in the chapter. After a broader understanding is achieved, it is easier to determine what problems exist (if any), how they could have been avoided, and what the manager should do next to deal with them.

3. Emphasize the complexity of most leadership situations and the tradeoffs faced by managers in making choices. Encourage students to consider different interpretations of the case rather than quickly focusing on a single, narrow interpretation. Encourage students to look for multiple causes of problems, rather than a simple explanation. Students should try to understand why people acted the way they did in the case, rather than stereotyping them or looking for someone to blame for problems. Most of the cases depict managers with both strengths and weaknesses who are trying to do their job in a way they think is appropriate.

4. Just as there are seldom simple explanations for leadership problems, there are seldom guaranteed remedies. In cases describing a manager who was generally successful, ask students to consider ways to improve the approach used by the manager to make it even more successful, and ask students if there are some completely different approaches that may also be effective in that situation. In cases describing a manager who has gotten into trouble, ask students to consider whether the person has some strengths rather than focusing only on weaknesses.

5. Encourage students to be open to alternative viewpoints when discussing the cases. Remind them that the group discussion will be more successful if one or two people do not try to dominate it and impose their own ideas on the group. This guideline about being open minded also applies to the instructor. Different interpretations of a case provide an opportunity to demonstrate how people approach a problem with different assumptions, biases, and priorities.

6. Vary the membership of small discussion groups from one class session to the next so that students are exposed to different points of view.

7. Encourage students to relate the case to their own experiences. For example, ask students to describe examples of similar incidents they have experienced in current or previous jobs, or in other organizations in which they were members.

Investment Management Inc.

The purpose of this case is to provide a specific example of the typical pattern of managerial activities for a top executive in a large private or public organization. The student is asked to identify activities that reflect the aspects of managerial work discussed in Chapter 2. Students should read the case prior to class and answer the questions on it by themselves. After the case is analyzed, it should be discussed in class or in small groups. The discussion requires about 20 minutes.

1. What managerial roles are most evident in this case?

• Monitor role. Richardson is continually gathering information about the operations of the company by meeting with subordinates, reading reports, talking on the telephone, and attending meetings conducted by others.

• Disseminator role. Richardson answers questions posed by his boss, subordinates, subordinates of subordinates, and a potential customer.

• Disturbance handler role. Considerable time is spent dealing with problems such as the response to a letter received by the company lawyer, what to do about a problem employee, and whether to reconsider a decision made earlier.

• Resource allocator role. This role is enacted by making a to-do list, and by discussing (with subordinates) the schedule of operations and priorities for the day.

• Figurehead, spokesman and liaison roles. Richardson meets with the vice chairman of a firm that is a potential customer to discuss his firm's products and services. Richardson's subordinate has the knowledge to deal with the potential customer, but it is more impressive for a vice chairman to meet with another top executive rather than with a sales representative or sales manager.

In this short description of managerial activities, there is little clear evidence of the entrepreneur, negotiator, and leader roles. However, all of the managerial roles apply to any manager or administrator, and over a longer period of observation it is likely that they would also be evident in Richardson's behavior. The leader role is often combined with other roles, and the description of conversation between Richardson and subordinates is not detailed enough to determine how much he attempts to motivate and direct them by giving praise and criticism and by emphasizing key objectives, priorities, and values.

2. Explain how this case illustrates the research findings about the nature of managerial work.

The descriptive research found that managerial work is inherently hectic, varied, fragmented, reactive, disorderly, and political, with a predominance of oral communication and informal interactions. These characteristics of managerial work can be seen in the description of Richardson's activities. It was a hectic day with little time alone for thinking about issues or reflective planning; even his lunch time was used to accomplish work. Most of his interactions were brief (ten minutes or less), and Richardson continually shifted from one subject to another, and from important to trivial matters. Most of the interactions were not scheduled in advance. Most of Richardson's activities involved responding to questions and requests initiated by other people. The interactions often involved people outside of the immediate chain of command, such as peers, subordinates of subordinates, and outsiders, not just his immediate subordinates and his boss (the CEO). Many of the interactions involved discussion of non-business subjects, and humor was used to reduce tension and maintain good relations with people.

Acme Manufacturing Company

In this case students analyze the activities of a manager to identify effective and ineffective behavior. The analysis gives students an opportunity to identify weaknesses in time management and to propose remedies. The problems involve a variety of managerial functions, including delegation, planning, and monitoring. Students should read the case prior to class and answer the questions on it by themselves. After the case is analyzed, it should be discussed in class or in small groups. The discussion requires about 30 minutes.

1. What specific things did Steve do wrong, and what should have been done in each instance?

• Steve is late for work because he overslept. He should have been more careful to set a backup alarm or to have someone wake him.

• Steve wastes time socializing with George Summers when he is already late. He should have greeted him and passed on quickly without inviting a lengthy discussion of home remodeling.

• Steve forgot the staff meeting with his boss at 9:30. He should have written it in his calendar and looked at the calendar before work.

• Steve has a disorderly office and could not find important memos and work orders. He should maintain a better system of files and records.

• Steve delegated the rush order to a production supervisor (Lucy Adams) but did not monitor progress. Since he doesn't know what is happening with the rush order, he is not able to deal with any problems with it. He needs to have a system for monitoring progress on the tasks for which he is responsible, even when they are delegated to a subordinate.

• Steve does not know where Lucy Adams is. He should have his subordinate managers inform him (or his secretary) when they are leaving the work area and say where they can be reached in case of an emergency.

• Steve went to an important meeting unprepared. As a result, he failed to impress his boss and peers. Steve should review the agenda and background materials for important meetings and be prepared to make a meaningful contribution.

• Steve did not know about the appointment with Mr. Ferris. Steve, or his secretary, should put appointments like this one on his calendar.

• The meeting with Mr. Ferris was not productive, because Steve could not help him (Mr. Ferris needed to talk to an engineer). Steve should try to determine in advance why someone wants a meeting with him, and the agenda for a meeting should be clarified as soon as the meeting begins. Steve wasted two hours on a meeting that could have been handled in a few minutes in his office or held in the company cafeteria (especially if the engineer joined them for lunch) rather than in an outside restaurant with slow service.

• Steve concentrated on completing a production report that was less urgent than preparing quality figures for his boss. He should make a list of necessary activities with their priorities, and plan his time accordingly. If he were better organized, it is likely that Steve would seldom have to take work home.

• Steve spent more than an hour assembling the quality data for his boss. The task was urgent, but the time-consuming job of assembling the data was not difficult and should have been delegated to his assistant manager, or perhaps even to his secretary. Steve only needed to spend a few minutes to check the completed work and make sure it was done correctly before giving it to his boss.

• Steve wasted an hour attending a safety meeting that was not important when he had other things to do that were much more important. Unlike the earlier staff meeting, he was not required to attend the safety meeting and could have delegated this task to a subordinate qualified to handle it.

• Steve never did talk to Lucy about the rush order or get back to the Sales Vice President as he promised, thereby leaving a poor impression with a highly-placed executive. He should have had his secretary (or his assistant) arrange a meeting with Lucy as soon as she returned to the plant.

2. What should Steve do to become more effective as a manager?

Steve does not manage his time well. He is disorganized and messy, he does not plan his daily activities, he wastes time on activities that are not important, he forgets appointments and meetings, he does not delegate effectively, he does not monitor important activities for which he is responsible, he does not prepare for important meetings, and he fails to deliver on promises to important people. Steve needs to apply some of the principles of time management. Some specific suggestions are as follows:

• Make a list of short and long term objectives.

• Make a daily "to-do list" of required activities and activities relevant to the objectives, indicating priority and deadlines.

• Keep a calendar listing scheduled activities such as meetings, appointments, and deadlines on important reports and projects.

• Use the to-do list and calendar to help plan what activities should be done first and to schedule activities during the day.

• Delegate to qualified subordinates activities that are not critical, or that are important but require more time than he has available.

• Develop an information/reporting system to monitor projects, workflow, and delegated activities.

• Use the secretary to screen calls and visitors effectively.

• Organize files, records, and desktop so that important documents can be found easily.

Consolidated Products

The purpose of this case is to provide students with an opportunity to use the behavior concepts presented in Chapter 3. Students are asked to analyze a case in which two managers use opposite patterns of managerial behavior, and consider the implications for managerial effectiveness. The case provides an opportunity to compare a task-oriented leader with a person-oriented leader, however these two broad categories are not sufficient for understanding what behavior is needed to be effective as a plant manager in this company. The case provides an opportunity to encourage students to use more specific categories of managerial behavior and to examine the effect of these behaviors on multiple criteria including both short-term and long-term outcomes.

Students should read the case and answer the questions on it by themselves, either in class or as homework prior to class. After the case is analyzed, it should be discussed in class or in small groups. The discussion requires about 30 minutes.

1. Describe the managerial behavior of Ben and Phil, using the specific behavior categories from Yukl's taxonomy.

Ben was very concerned about employees and acted friendly and supportive towards them. His concern was reflected in his efforts to protect employee jobs and make the work environment more pleasant. He socialized with employees and maintained an extensive network of personal friendships. However, Ben had a relatively weak concern for productivity and product quality. He was satisfied to maintain the same level of production, and he did not set high performance objectives and quality standards. He delegated the responsibility for supervising employees entirely to his first-line supervisors. In terms of the Yukl taxonomy, there is evidence that Ben used supporting and some aspects of delegating, team building, and networking; he made little use of clarifying, planning, problem solving, monitoring, and motivating.

In contrast to Ben, Phil was very concerned about the task. Phil set high performance standards, pressured people to achieve them, and checked closely on their performance. He was very directive and autocratic in making decisions. However, Phil had little concern for employees. He did not hesitate to make decisions that cut costs at the expense of employee benefits and jobs. In terms of the Yukl taxonomy, there is evidence that Phil used clarifying, planning, problem solving, monitoring, and some aspects of motivating (use of coercion); he was low on supporting, delegating, consulting, and team building.

2. Compare the two managers in terms of their influence on employee attitudes and performance.

Due to the extensive use of employee-oriented behavior by Ben, employees were satisfied with the company, as evidenced by the very low turnover in his plant. However, employees were not highly motivated, and they did not perform up to their capacity. Ben's plant had the second worst performance of the company's five plants.

Phil's lack of concern for employees was reflected in growing dissatisfaction and increased turnover among the supervisors and machine operators. Phil had a very short-term perspective on plant performance, which resulted in cutting expenses for development of human resources and maintenance of machines. He is the type of manager who makes a good initial impression based on the short-term indicators of financial performance, such as quarterly costs and production levels. However, the longer-term effectiveness of the work unit will suffer, due to the decline in human and material resources. Unfortunately, by the time the delayed, adverse effects of Phil's actions become evident, he is likely be promoted and off to another position, leaving the mess for his successor to face.

3. If you were the manager of this plant, what would you do to achieve both high employee satisfaction and performance?

A better balance of task and relationship behavior is needed. The plant manager should be supportive toward employees but also exhibit task-oriented behaviors such as setting challenging objectives, planning improvement in productivity and quality, and monitoring performance to ensure progress is being made toward achieving these objectives. It is better to delegate responsibility to supervisors (as Ben did) than to make all important decisions in an autocratic manner (as Phil did), but delegation without clear objectives and standards is ineffective. There was no evidence that either manager used important behaviors such as recognizing and rewarding effective performance, developing subordinate skills, consulting with subordinates, and inspiring a strong sense of commitment to task objectives (motivating). Finally, investment in developing human resources and maintenance of physical resources are important for long-term objectives and should not be sacrificed for temporary gains in short-term objectives.

Air Force Supply Squadron

Like the preceding case, this one gives students an opportunity to use the behavior concepts presented in Chapter 3. The case provides an example of an effective military leader who uses a variety of different managerial behaviors. Students should read the case and answer the questions on it by themselves, either in class or as homework. After the case is analyzed, it should be discussed in class or in small groups. The discussion requires about 20 minutes.

1. What types of managerial behaviors did Colonel Novak exhibit?

Evidence of several managerial behaviors can be found in this case:

• Motivating and inspiring. In his initial meeting with the men in his squadron Colonel Novak made a speech in which he talked about the importance of the mission to the war effort and the importance of each man's job. He also set an example of dedication (role modeling) by pitching in to help with manual work to load supplies desperately needed at the front lines.

• Supporting. Colonel Novak showed a personal interest in his men. He visited with the men on and off duty, learned their names, learned something about their backgrounds, listened to their complaints, and tried to deal with their concerns about poor living conditions on the base.

• Clarifying and informing. Colonel Novak assigned responsibilities to each officer, delegated authority clearly to reduce confusion and avoid duplication of orders. The frequent staff meetings were a way to ensure that officers were better informed about the operations of the squadron and about decisions, plans, and responsibilities.

• Planning and organizing. Colonel Novak reorganized the squadron to place people where the best use could be made of their skills and experience.

• Monitoring. Colonel Novak held frequent meetings with his officers to find out about the operations of the squadron, he met with the enlisted men to find out about their concerns and complaints, and he flew along with the airplane crews to learn how the supply operations were being conducted.

• Consulting and delegating. Colonel Novak met with his officers to discuss the methods used to carry out the mission of the squadron. He delegated more authority to the non-commissioned officers to direct and supervise their men and supported most of their decisions.

• Conflict management. Colonel Novak used staff meetings to discuss disagreements among the officers and resolve them, and he assigned key responsibilities when all concerned were present to avoid any misunderstandings about who was responsible for what.

In this brief case description there was little or no direct evidence that Novak used problem solving, rewarding, recognizing, developing, or networking. However, it is quite likely that he also used some or all of these managerial behaviors to some extent.

2. What does this case illustrate about effective leadership?

Effective leaders use a variety of managerial behaviors that reflect a dual concern for task objectives and interpersonal relationships. Colonel Novak was clearly concerned about accomplishing the mission of his squadron, as evidenced by his efforts to reorganize it, clarify roles and responsibilities, and find better ways to do the work. However, Novak also knew that it would not be possible to accomplish their mission without improving morale, helping the men to manage the stress, reducing interpersonal conflict, and getting the men to work together as a team.

Sterling Products

The purpose of this case is to provide students with an example of a typical problem that occurs when two interdependent functions or departments fail to coordinate their plans. Students have an opportunity to analyze the case and identify examples of ineffective behavior by the marketing vice president, the production vice president, and the CEO. Students should read the case and answer the questions on it by themselves, either in class or as homework. After the case is analyzed, it should be discussed in class or in small groups. The discussion requires about 20 minutes.

1. What mistakes did each of the three executives make in this case?

The problems in this case are due primarily to poor planning and lack of coordination. Neither vice president could accomplish his or her objectives without the cooperation and support of the other vice president. However, instead of cooperation, the two vice presidents pursue incompatible strategies. We don't have enough information to know which strategy is best, but neither has much hope of succeeding without a coordinated effort.

The marketing vice president should not have made and implemented plans to increase orders for the premier product without first ensuring that enough production would be available to fill these new orders. Some sort of tentative arrangement had been made to purchase new machines to make the premier brand, but these plans were never finalized and confirmed. Moreover, the marketing vice president needed to determine more accurately what product costs would be before making pricing decisions and estimating potential profits from sales for each brand. It was not enough to send a memo with sales forecasts to the production vice president. Written communications are not sufficient for handling this type of situation. Face-to-face interaction is more appropriate for gathering information and making influence attempts to elicit cooperation, especially from someone who doubts that the sales forecasts are realistic.

The production vice president should have conferred with the marketing vice president to make sure their objectives for the coming year were compatible. The production vice president should not have assumed that the sales force would push the economy brand after it became possible to price it more competitively. Tentative plans to use available funds to purchase machines for the premier brand should not have been changed without first consulting with the marketing vice president and the CEO. The memo about costs for the economy brand failed to communicate the production vice president's expectations and did not include any information about costs for the premier brand. Again, written memos are not the best way to resolve conflicts and ensure cooperation.

It is the primary responsibility of the CEO to ensure that subunit plans are compatible with each other and with the overall strategies and objectives for the company. In this case, the CEO appears to favor the strategy of cutting prices on the economy brand, but apparently did not inform the marketing vice president or consult with her about possible alternative strategies that may be more promising. Fred did not make any effort to ensure that the two vice presidents were committed to a common strategy, and he did not monitor events in the company closely enough to detect the problems before they became serious. Fred should have talked more frequently with his vice presidents. If it was not feasible to monitor events closely when he went overseas, Fred should have designated someone to assume responsibility in his absence for managing the day-to-day operations of the company.

2. What things could have been done to avoid these problems and increase the likelihood of achieving higher company profits?

The problems could have been avoided by the use of a joint planning process that involves all of the key parties meeting together to reach agreement on strategies for the organization. Even after reaching initial agreement, continued consultation is necessary as more detailed plans are formulated by each unit, to ensure that efforts will be coordinated and necessary support and cooperation from other units will be obtained. The CEO should have ensured that everyone was in agreement about objectives, priorities, and initial plans for achieving them before departing on a lengthy foreign trip. During his trip, Fred should have monitored progress occasionally by means of progress review discussions with each vice president. If problems arose that required joint resolution, the CEO could have used a conference call with both vice presidents simultaneously.

3. What should Fred Anderson do now?

Fred needs to implement a better procedure for strategic planning for Sterling Products in which the two vice presidents share in the responsibility for the overall company strategy rather than focusing exclusively on their own subunit. The executive team should meet to plan strategy jointly, clarify priorities among the different products, and ensure that everybody understands and is committed to the new objectives and strategies. The type of communication breakdown and confusion illustrated in the case can be avoided in the future by the type of process just described. All three executives made mistakes and are partly responsible for the strategy fiasco. Fred's orientation should be to learn from the mistakes and avoid repeating them in the future, not to look for someone to blame.

Reliable Taxicab Company

This case demonstrates the importance of taking into account the attitudes and perceptions of people as well as mechanical things when developing and implementing solutions to technological problems. The case describes the initial failure and eventual success of a maintenance manager's efforts to implement a new preventative maintenance program in a taxi company. Students should read the case and answer the questions on it by themselves, either in class or as homework. After the case is analyzed, it should be discussed in class or in small groups. The discussion requires about 20 minutes.

1. Why was Michelle's initial approach for reducing taxi breakdowns unsuccessful?

In her analysis of the reasons for taxi breakdowns, Michelle discovered that many breakdowns could be avoided if the taxi drivers reported early signs of mechanical problems. She attempted to implement a new program in preventative maintenance in which drivers would fill out a detailed report when they suspected any mechanical problem in their taxi. She relied on an impersonal memo to the drivers to gain their cooperation. This is a typical engineering solution that underestimates the importance of cooperation by the humans who must implement it. Most of the drivers resisted doing the reports, because they viewed them as a paperwork exercise that was unnecessary and a waste of their time. Even when they suspected that their taxi had a mechanical problem, they could drive it until the problem was so obvious that it did not require the new paperwork to be fixed.

The resistance of the drivers may also reflect doubts about Michelle's expertise as a maintenance supervisor, which in the past was traditionally a male job. The drivers did not have much opportunity to learn about her qualifications, because she was relatively new to the position and seldom interacted with them on a face-to-face basis. After a few weeks of noncooperation from the drivers, Michelle tried two other ways to influence cooperation. She asked the dispatchers (who talked to the drivers frequently) to encourage driver cooperation, and she sent another memo warning about the serious consequences of field breakdowns. Neither approach was successful. Perhaps the dispatchers also resisted cooperating with her, or perhaps they just did not have much influence with the drivers. Moreover, Michelle did not have any power to discipline drivers who failed to cooperate.

2. Why was the final approach more successful in getting cooperation from the taxi drivers?

Michelle used some forms of monitoring and informing behavior to gain the cooperation of the drivers. First, she met with some of the drivers to find out how they perceived the maintenance forms. When she discovered that they perceived the reports as busywork, she began sending followup memos thanking a driver for filling out the report and explaining what mechanical problems were found and what was done about them. This feedback was a way of keeping the drivers informed about her actions and showing that the reports were taken seriously.

3. What other things could Michelle have done to improve cooperation by the taxi drivers?

• Michelle could have made more of an effort to get to know the drivers on a personal basis whenever there was an opportunity. For example, she could have positioned herself at locations frequented by the drivers to talk with them, and she could have held some meetings with the drivers and dispatchers to talk about ways to improve customer service.

• Michelle could have used some of the other influence tactics described in Chapter 8, such as rational persuasion, exchange, and inspirational appeals to gain the commitment of the drivers to the preventative maintenance program. These tactics would be more effective if used in a meeting with drivers rather than in a written memo.

• Michelle could have held meetings with the drivers to discuss the problem of breakdowns and jointly develop some solutions (this is a form of consultation). Some of the drivers may have suggested the preventative maintenance program, and if not, she could have suggested it as one of the solutions to be considered by the group. As discussed in Chapter 6, people are likely to be more committed to implement a program that they help to develop.

American Financial Corporation

This case demonstrates the importance of carefully monitoring an important assignment with a tight deadline. The case provides students with an opportunity to identify typical mistakes in monitoring activities and conducting progress review meetings. The case also allows students to assess their understanding of guidelines for scheduling progress reviews and their knowledge of appropriate procedures for dealing with performance problems discovered during monitoring. Students should read the case and answer the questions on it by themselves, either in class or as homework. After the case is analyzed, it should be discussed in class or in small groups. The discussion requires about 20 minutes.

1. What did Betty do wrong prior to the meeting, and what could have been done to avoid missing the deadline?

The appropriate amount of monitoring depends on the complexity of an assignment, the likelihood of serious problems, and the reliability of the subordinate. Since Don had missed deadlines before this, Betty should have been aware of the need for careful monitoring. At least one progress check was needed about midway through the project to make sure there were no problems or unforeseen complications. Moreover, Betty should have set a deadline that would allow enough time to review the report and make sure it was ready for the vice president. Unfortunately, Betty never checked to see how the project was going. She failed to check on the report prior to leaving on a trip, and she did not return Don's call when she was away, which would have let her know about the problem earlier.

In addition, Betty should have asked Don to develop a brief action plan indicating key action steps and who would be responsible for each one. Betty should have met with Don soon after she made the assignment to review his action plan. Most likely a discussion of action plans would have made it clear that the figures should be checked for accuracy and completeness before doing the analysis, and would have raised the issue of Don's need for more clerical support.

It is important to note that Don is highly motivated to do good quality work, but he needs some help in planning how to get assignments done on time. His compulsiveness may be making it difficult for him to delegate appropriate parts of a task. It is part of Betty's responsibility as a supervisor to help Don develop better planning skills and to learn how to delegate and manage his time better.

2. What did Betty do wrong in the meeting itself, and what could have been done to make the meeting more effective?

The immediate problem facing Betty is how to get the report done properly and quickly. Instead of focusing on this objective, Betty becomes preoccupied with criticizing Don and blaming him for the delays. She should take a problem solving approach and determine what needs to be done to complete the report. She is part of the cause of the problem, and this is not the time to be finding fault.

In the meeting Betty does some things that are ineffective for reviewing progress and dealing with performance problems. She is sarcastic and insulting, she interrupts Don when he tries to explain what happened, she gets into other issues (messy office) that are not relevant to the immediate problem, and she makes threats that are not necessary to influence him to finish the report.

3. How are aspects of planning, monitoring, informing, and problem solving woven together in this case?

This case shows how different types of managerial behavior are interrelated. When an assignment is made, the subordinate should be informed about the objectives, the deadline for completion, and the priorities for different aspects of the work. Next, the subordinate should make preliminary action plans. These action plans should be reviewed by the manager to ensure that they are feasible and consistent with his or her own plans. The action planning provides a basis for making resource allocation decisions to ensure adequate support for a task, and it may reveal whether a subordinate needs more advice or guidance on how to handle the task. Moreover, identification of key action steps provides checkpoints to facilitate monitoring by the manager. Monitoring facilitates early detection of problems and corrective action to deal with them before they become more serious. Accurate upward informing by a subordinate supplements monitoring by the manager. In this case, there was little downward monitoring or upward informing, and the manager did not know there was a problem until it was too late to avoid undesirable outcomes.

Rejected Plans

The purpose of this case is to provide an example of supportive communication and active listening involving a co-worker who is upset and frustrated. The supportive behavior illustrated in this case is equally applicable to subordinates, peers, or even a superior. Students should read the case and answer the questions on it by themselves, either in class or as homework. After the case is analyzed, it should be discussed in class or in small groups. The discussion requires about 20 minutes.

1. Describe examples of effective behavior by Ellen.

• Ellen used restatement to test for comprehension and encourage further explanation.

> Things must not have gone as well as you hoped they would.

> You mean he didn't accept any of them?

> After all the effort you put into those plans, you still couldn't figure out whether Peterson was rejecting you or your plans, right?

> Sure. If he said your plans were unrealistic, what does that mean? . . . It's just too general . . . meaningless, even.

• Ellen showed empathy for feelings or attitudes not directly expressed.

> It looks as if you're pretty upset about it.

> I'll bet it does. I would be upset too.

> I can understand the confusion and uncertainty that were caused when you felt Peterson's actions were unreasonable.

> Yet, in the back of your mind, you probably figured that Peterson wouldn't risk the company's future just because he didn't like you personally.

• Ellen used probes to encourage Bob to say more about what happened.

> What did he say about them?

> Did you ask him to point out some problems or explain the reasons for his rejection more clearly?

• Ellen showed respect for Bob's ability, thereby helping to reduce defensiveness and encourage consideration of the possibility that the plans were rejected for reasons other than being inadequate.

> Bob, you do such good work, it's hard for me to figure out why your plans were rejected by Peterson.

• Ellen helped Bob to recognize that Peterson's rejection of the plans may have been due to other, less threatening, reasons besides personal dislike of Bob.

> Maybe he didn't understand the plans, or maybe it was just his off day.

• Ellen was very tactful when she encouraged Bob to talk to Peterson again to learn more about his reasons for rejecting Bob's plans. The suggestion was put as a question ("Do you think it would help to . . .") so that she did not appear to be telling him what he should do.

2. Do you think most managers would have handled this incident the same way Ellen did?

The way Ellen handled this incident appears obvious to readers. Nevertheless, her response represents an unusually high level of skill in active listening and supportive counseling. Many managers would likely express sympathy at Bob's plight without listening carefully or attempting to help him deal with his personal problem. Some managers would try to provide counseling, but tell Bob what he should do rather than helping him develop his own solution.

3. How was Bob's perception affected by Peterson's style of communication?

Peterson was very evaluative in reacting to Bob's plans. He made a blanket rejection ("they are unrealistic and too difficult to implement") without providing specific details about weaknesses and without noting any positive aspects. This style of evaluation by Peterson caused Bob to be a very angry and frustrated, which prevented Bob from probing to discover the reasons for the rejection.

Computer Peripherals Inc.

The purpose of this case is to provide students with an example of process consultation behavior that can be used to help resolve a conflict between two parties. This type of conflict management intervention is powerful and is not difficult to use. Students should read the case and answer the questions on it by themselves, either in class or as homework. After the case is analyzed, it should be discussed in class or in small groups. The discussion requires about 20 minutes.

1. Describe examples of effective behaviors by Gary in dealing with the conflict.

• He made it clear right away to both parties that he thought the conflict was a serious problem and explained why it was important to resolve it.

• He explained his role in trying to help resolve the conflict.

• He asked each party to explain what the other is doing that is bothersome. Just talking about one's anger often helps a person dissipate some of the anger, and the focus on specific actions that are annoying provides useful feedback to the other party.

• He encouraged active listening by disallowing interruptions and requiring restatement of what the other person said. This is an important element of process consultation, because each party views the conflict in widely discrepant ways. For example, Tony perceived Laird as needlessly compulsive about quality, whereas Tony saw Laird as indifferent about quality; in both cases the perception was distorted.

• He thanked Tony for being candid.

• He emphasized the progress being made in improving understanding.

• He asked each person to indicate some actions the person would take to improve relations.

• He set a date to check on progress after an appropriate interval of time.

2. Evaluate the likely success of the intervention.

The conflict management intervention illustrated in this case incorporates features found in other effective approaches for resolving conflicts, such as establishing a supportive climate, listening to each party impartially without taking sides, discovering how each party perceives the conflict, encouraging each party to listen carefully to the other party without being defensive, identifying causes of the conflict, getting each party to commit to concrete action steps for reducing conflict, and monitoring the process. The process consultation intervention went smoothly. Each person seemed to learn something about how the other perceived him. Each acknowledged some responsibility for the bad feelings and promised to improve some specific behaviors contributing to the conflict. Thus, some improvement in relations is likely to occur.

3. What other techniques or approaches could have been used to manage the conflict?

The intervention used by Gary is likely to be fairly successful without any other techniques, but some other approaches were feasible, either in combination with the intervention used or in place of it.

• Gary could have investigated whether there was a more substantive basis for the conflict. For example, there may be a lack of clarity about the relative priority of objectives such as product quality and quantity; if so, there may be need for a clearer statement of priorities by higher management. Perhaps Laird's suggestions about improving quality are viewed as infeasible (if he does more to improve quality, quantity may suffer), or perhaps Tony resents having his actions second guessed by someone who is a peer in another department.

• Gary could have examined other possible sources of conflict such as jurisdictional ambiguity, communication barriers, competition for resources, and so forth. If any of these conditions was found to contribute substantially to the conflict, Gary could change the conditions.

• Gary could have encouraged the subordinates to identify common values and interests before examining differences and points of disagreement.

• Gary could have asked each person to describe his own intentions and behavior. The addition of this step would permit a more elaborate process consultation procedure wherein each subordinate examines differences between self-perceptions and the perception of the other person, and also differences between perception of the other person and the other person's self-perception.

• Gary could have encouraged his subordinates to focus on behavior rather than making accusations about personality, such as calling someone "sneaky" and "power hungry." It is a matter of choice, but some theorists prefer to avoid personality issues unless absolutely necessary to understand the conflict.

• As a possible structural change to encourage closer cooperation between departments on quality issues, Gary could establish a quality committee ("quality circle") composed of employees from both departments. The committee would meet regularly to discuss ways to improve product quality, and their recommendations would be reviewed by a management committee consisting of Gary, Tony, and Laird.

• Gary could have simply ordered Tony and Laird to cooperate with each other more. However, this approach is likely to be less successful than process consultation, because the subordinates did not understood each other's perceptions and did not know what to do to reduce the conflict.

Universal Widgets

The case describes an interaction between a manager and a subordinate who comes to discuss a problem. The purpose of this case is to provide an example of effective managerial behavior for active listening and coaching. Students should read the case and answer the questions on it by themselves, either in class or as homework. After the case is analyzed, it should be discussed in class or in small groups. The discussion requires about 20 minutes.

1. Describe examples of effective managerial behaviors by Joy.

Joy provides coaching that will help Tom learn how to handle the problem himself. In general she asks him to explain how he plans to deal with the problem, asks probing questions to get him to consider important aspects of the problem that he may have overlooked, asks him to identify different options, and acknowledges good ideas and proposals. In handling this interaction Joy demonstrates her skill in active listening, which is an important part of coaching. Some specific examples of effective behavior are the following:

• When Tom describes the problem, she probes for more details. She is continually asking Tom specific questions about what he has done, how he perceives the situation, and what he plans to do next.

• When Tom asks her whether she agrees that it is wise to avoid a confrontation with Dan, she is careful to avoid a simple yes or no answer and instead helps Dan to make an analysis of the situation.

• When Tom asks Joy to talk to Ted's boss as a way to influence Ted, she asks probing questions to encourage Tom to identify some better options for gaining Ted's cooperation. She encourages Tom to analyze Ted's interests to find ways to persuade him to accept lower tolerances.

• When she wants to suggest something for Tom to do, she words it in the form of a question ("Do you suppose it would help to emphasize the company's theme of dependable service?")

2. What would a manager who is not oriented toward developing subordinates likely do in this situation?

The managerial behavior in this case is deceptively simple, but most managers would probably not handle the situation in this way. A typical response when subordinates come to the manager with a problem is to tell them how to deal with it. Even when a subordinate has been assigned responsibility for handling a particular issue, most managers tend to perceive themselves as having more expertise than the subordinate. They may give advice as a way to demonstrate their superiority, or because they believe the subordinate really needs and wants their advice. It takes a special effort to avoid the natural tendency to be directive when talking to a subordinate (a similar problem occurs for a parent in dealing with a teenage child). Unless a manager is oriented toward developing subordinates, he or she is unlikely to take the kind of developmental approach demonstrated by Joy in this case.

Echo Electronics

The purpose of this case is to provide students with a better understanding of the potential benefits of participative leadership. Students are asked to read a case describing a decision for which an autocratic decision was unsuccessful. The mistakes made by the manager in this case demonstrate the importance of consultation in making decisions that have important implications both for subordinates and the organization. Students should read the case prior to class and answer the questions on it by themselves. After the case is analyzed, it should be discussed in class or in small groups. The discussion requires about 30 minutes.

1. What actions could Paul have taken to prevent the problem?

Use of participative leadership by Paul may have prevented this problem. Consultation with employees about major changes is useful for discovering potential resistance to the change, gaining commitment to it, and getting suggestions on ways to implement the change more effectively. A major change in the work such as introduction of new equipment can have a very disruptive effect on people. The new workstations may be perceived by the workers either as an improvement or a threat. The new workstations may be viewed as providing a number of advantages, such as making the work more interesting, raising the skill level of employees, and providing an opportunity to increase productivity and product quality, thereby making the company more competitive and protecting the jobs of workers. Conversely, the workers may perceive the new equipment as a threat to their job security, because fewer workers will be needed when productivity is increased. Moreover, workers who are not computer literate may be anxious about learning new skills and worried that their experience and technical skills will become obsolete in the new computerized factory.

A major change of this type should be introduced carefully and slowly to avoid negative reactions. The potential benefits for the company and the workers should have been explained before the changes were made, and the supervisors and workers should have been invited to participate in meetings to plan how to implement the changes effectively. Employees should have been encouraged to express any concerns and doubts about the feasibility of the proposed changes. The opportunity to discuss changes and influence them reduces anxiety and helps to avoid false rumors. Whenever possible, Paul should have modified the planned changes to deal with employee concerns and utilize good employee suggestions, thereby giving the employees (and the supervisors) a sense of ownership of the changes.

A number of other things could have been done to ensure that the new workstations would be viewed as a positive change. These actions do not involve participative management, but they help create a climate of trust and security in which participation will be more effective. Paul could have tried to persuade top management to guarantee that no jobs would be lost as a result of the change. Paul should have tried to find some ways for the workers to benefit from the changes, for example, by earning more after learning new skills needed to operate the workstations. Paul should have made sure that the workers were provided adequate training to help them learn how to operate the new machines effectively.

2. What steps should Paul take now to deal with the problem?

The first step is to determine the cause of the problem. It is not clear why productivity and quality decreased. Paul's four supervisors disagree about the cause, and they have little evidence to support their opinions.

There does not appear to be a deficiency in the equipment, but more investigation is needed to completely rule out this possibility. Paul needs more information about the timing, scope, and intensity of the problem. He should determine whether productivity and quality has declined for all of the workers, or only for some workers, for some departments, or for some shifts. If the company has a good information system, this type of information can be assembled quickly. To evaluate the intensity of the problem and the possibility of other causes unrelated to the workstations (e.g., a long-term decline in worker satisfaction, deficiencies in materials used in the production process), Paul should examine data for the two years prior to the introduction of workstations to see if the pattern was one of stable, increasing, or decreasing productivity and quality. Paul also needs to check with his contacts in other companies using the workstations to determine whether they also experienced a decline in productivity and quality during the first few months after the workstations were introduced (perhaps due to a natural part of the learning curve).

There is some evidence to suggest that the problem is due at least in part to worker resistance. Worker morale has declined, and two employees quit because they were upset about changes in how the work is done. These reactions suggest that many of the workers may view the new workstations as a threat rather than a benefit, but Paul needs more information to confirm this diagnosis. He should hold meetings with groups of workers to discuss the new workstations and learn how the workers feel about them. If the workers trust Paul, it should be possible to discover their concerns and complaints.

It would be helpful to know whether low worker morale was precipitated by the introduction of new equipment or was already present (due to other causes) and was only aggravated by the changes. Information about the underlying attitudes and values of the workers is needed to evaluate the feasibility of various approaches for dealing with the problem of the workstations. For example, Paul needs to determine the extent to which the workers share the objectives of improving productivity and/or quality. If workers care about these objectives, Paul can invite them to participate in finding ways to make the new workstations successful as a means improving quality and productivity.

In his investigation of the problem, Paul may find that it has multiple causes, each of which requires a different type of solution. If the workers were not properly trained to operate the new equipment, then new training should be developed quickly. If the new workstations have made the job less satisfying for the workers, then the job should be redesigned to make it more interesting and fulfilling. If the workers are afraid that the new machines will erode their job security, then Paul needs to provide assurances that no jobs will be lost as a result of increased productivity. If management has failed to provide any benefits to workers for making the change successful, then Paul should propose some new benefits such as higher pay for more skill. In his plan to deal with the problem, it may be necessary for Paul to propose changes in such things as compensation, job design, work rules, job security, or training procedures and persuade the CEO that they are necessary. One advantage Paul has is the fact that the CEO approved the initial plan for the change and shares part of the responsibility for its deficiencies.

Alvis Corporation

The purpose of this case is to provide students with a better understanding of the potential pitfalls of participative leadership. Students are asked to read a case describing two decisions for which a participative approach was unsuccessful. The mistakes made by the manager in this case demonstrate the importance of leader skill in making difficult decisions involving inherent conflicts of interest. Students should read the case prior to class and answer the questions on it by themselves. After the case is analyzed, it should be discussed in class or in small groups. The discussion requires about 30 minutes.

1. Were the two decisions suitable ones for a group decision procedure?

In the decision about production standards, decision quality is clearly important, because low standards cost the company more in incentive pay. Acceptance is also important, because the incentive system will not be effective if workers believe management is trying to exploit them. Production quality is already a problem, and it would likely get worse if workers become very frustrated and angry over the handling of the incentives. Kevin has the information necessary to make a high quality decision, but an autocratic decision to raise production standards risks decision acceptance. Workers do not want cuts in their incentive pay, whereas the leader is expected by top management to reduce labor costs. The most appropriate procedure for this type of decision is probably consultation. Kevin used a group decision, which risks decision quality, because worker objectives are not congruent with the organization's objectives.

In the vacation decision, decision quality is moderately important; the workers are not interchangeable in terms of their job skills, and different ways of setting up the vacation schedule have different implications for department performance. Decision acceptance is also important, since some workers feel strongly about taking their vacation at a particular time. Kevin lacks some of the information needed to make the decision, such as his subordinates' preferences for different vacation times. However, once he has this information, he can make a high quality decision by himself. Finally, it is likely that subordinate objectives are not entirely congruent with the leader's objectives to maintain department performance. The most appropriate procedure for this type of decision is consultation. Kevin used a group decision, which risks decision quality if the workers decide on a schedule that leaves some essential jobs without adequate coverage.

Consultation with individuals is a better procedure for making the vacation scheduling decision than simultaneous consultation with the entire group. Kevin could start by asking each worker to indicate preferred weeks on a calendar or form. Then he could see if there was a schedule that would provide adequate job coverage and still satisfy everyone. If no simple solution was evident, he could meet with only the few workers who want the same vacation period to see if the matter could be resolved to everyone's satisfaction. If no agreement is possible, Kevin has a variety of options. He could continue to use productivity as the criterion for deciding among people who want the same vacation period, or he could resort to some type of chance procedure such as flipping a coin or letting people draw numbers that indicate their order of choice (i.e., person who draws the "1" gets first choice, person who draws a "2" gets second choice, etc.).

2. What mistakes did Kevin make in using participation, and what could have been done to avoid the difficulties he encountered?

A group decision was not the recommended procedure for making the two decisions, but even if it had been, Kevin made some major mistakes in using this procedure. He should have stayed with the group to serve as the discussion leader and facilitator. For the vacation decision he should have made it clear to the group that the options are limited to ones providing coverage for essential tasks. In the case of the decision about production standards, it is essential to introduce the issues in a way that encourages and facilitates constructive problem solving rather than polarization between workers and management.

The decision about production standards illustrates the importance of proper timing in use of decision procedures. The adjustment of production standards should have been made before the new equipment was installed. It would have been easier to reach a satisfactory agreement before workers became accustomed to receiving the higher incentive pay. Even if information about productivity gains was insufficient to determine exactly what the standards should be, some tentative arrangements should have been made so that workers would clearly expect the standards to be adjusted. Then after some experience with the new equipment, Kevin could consult with the workers about making any necessary adjustments.

3. Were these decisions appropriate ones for introducing participation into Kevin's department?

The two decisions are a poor choice for introducing participative management into Kevin's department. It is best to begin with an issue that does not involve inherent conflicts among employees, or between employees and management. The incentive pay decision involves an inherent conflict between the workers and management over division of the benefits from higher productivity; the workers want a share of the benefits, but management wants to use all the benefits to pay for the new equipment. The vacation schedule decision involves a conflict among various individuals who want to take their vacations at the same time and disagree about the appropriate criteria for deciding who gets their preferred time.

An example of a more suitable issue for introducing participation is how to improve product quality. High quality products and services is an objective that can be embraced by all members of the organization, especially when quality is a strong value in the organization culture.

4. What should Kevin do now?

There is no obvious easy answer, but the issue of quality improvement provides a possible way out of Kevin's current dilemma over the issue of the pay incentives. It is expensive to scrap or rework defective equipment, and if defective equipment is sold to customers, the result can be returned goods or loss of future sales. Participation by the workers in developing work procedures that improve both quality and efficiency would increase the amount of benefits to be divided between workers and management, thereby making it easier to find a mutually acceptable solution. One promising approach for Kevin is to explain the conflict situation to the workers and ask them to join him in finding a solution that would satisfy everyone. For this approach to work, however, Kevin must also gain the cooperation of top management. With regard to the vacation schedule decision, the best approach is probably for Kevin to acknowledge that this decision is best handled by consulting with individuals, at least until a later time when the group becomes more skilled in dealing with this type of conflict.

The 60-hour Week

The purpose of this case is to provide students with an opportunity to see specific examples of delegation by a first-line supervisor. The case demonstrates both effective and ineffective behaviors. It is a very simple case, but the concrete examples of delegation behavior are useful for students with little or no work experience. Students should read the case and answer the questions on it by themselves, either in class or as homework. After the case is analyzed, it should be discussed in class or in small groups. The discussion requires about 20 minutes.

1. What are some examples of effective behavior by Marvin in delegating responsibilities to Sylvia, Jane, and Pam?

• He delegated tasks that are fairly routine and not central to the manager's role.

• He delegated tasks that are appropriate for the ability and confidence of subordinates.

• He specified new responsibilities to each subordinate and explained why the task was important.

• He checked for comprehension by asking if there were any questions.

• He provided adequate authority and resources. In the case of Jane, he arranged a partitioned office to ensure privacy.

• He made some effort to ensure that subordinates accepted the new responsibilities. For example, with his secretary, he asked her if she would mind writing the customer letters herself. Acceptance did not appear to be an issue for Sylvia and Jane.

• When his secretary made a mistake, he discussed the reasons in a calm and helpful manner and made it a learning experience for both of them. In this type of situation, some managers would have withdrawn responsibility for the task, but he appropriately avoided this pitfall and demonstrated his continued confidence in Pam.

2. What mistakes were made by Marvin when he delegated the letter writing to his secretary?

• When initially delegating the task, he did not clarify the importance of checking the files before writing to a customer regarding overdue payment.

• He did not specify reporting requirements and monitor progress carefully in the early stages of delegation for any of his subordinates. In the case of his secretary, an embarrassing mistake was made because he did not check to see if she was doing the letters correctly.

3. Is the delegation to the three subordinates likely to be effective?

Yes. The subordinates appear competent and should be able to do their new tasks as well as Marvin did. Marvin's special assignment overloaded him and made it necessary to consider more delegation, but even before this time, more delegation would have been appropriate. Rather than spending so much time on operating work, Marvin should have been doing more managerial work, such as planning and developing subordinates.

Restview Hospital

The purpose of this case is to develop more skill in analyzing power relations and understanding how upward information power and exclusive access to decision makers may be used to influence organizational decisions. The case also illustrates how poor decisions may be reached by top management even when there is objective evidence available to make a more rational decision. Students should read the case and answer the questions on it by themselves, either in class or as homework. After the case is analyzed, it should be discussed in class or in small groups. The discussion requires about 20 minutes.

1. How would you explain the board's decision to purchase the software package from Standard?

The board acted on the information that was available to it. It is likely that Jack distorted the information to favor the decision to purchase the software package from his friend's company. He did not allow Mary to make a presentation to the board, he did not allow them to see her report, and he discouraged Mary from inviting them to the vendor presentations. It was probably not necessary for Jack to argue that Standard's software package was superior to the others, only that the various software packages were equally suitable for Restview Hospital. The argument to reward Standard Software for their excellent customer service in the past would seem like a reasonable justification as long as the competing software packages were not otherwise different in price or suitability.

2. How much power relative to this decision did Mary, Jack, and the president of Standard Software possess, and what type of power was it?

Jack had information power derived from his exclusive control over dissemination of information about the suitability of the different software packages. He also had some expert power as the facility administrator who successfully managed the installation of other computer systems in the past. To the board, Jack appeared as the person with the most expertise about the decision. Jack also had position power over Mary, and could use this power to encourage her to include Standard Software among the vendors selected for final consideration, to discourage her from inviting board members to the vendor presentations, and to discourage her from attending the board meeting. It is not clear how much expert and referent power Jack had over Mary before the decision was made, but it is likely that his referent power with her was reduced by the underhanded way he influenced the decision. His expert power with Mary and others in the company was probably reduced after the decision proved to be a poor one, unless he was able to shift the blame to someone else (e.g., Mary).

Mary's greater knowledge about the various software systems did not translate into expert power with Jack, because this expertise was not relevant to his concerns. It is not clear how much expert power Mary had with the board of directors. Jack may have mentioned to them that Mary participated in the evaluation process, but it is doubtful that they knew Mary had more knowledge about the subject than Jack did. There is little information in the case to determine how much referent power Mary had with either Jack or the board.

The president of Standard Software obviously had considerable referent power over Jack, and this may have been the sole basis for influencing Jack to purchase Standard's softward package. However, it is possible that Jack was also influenced by the president's considerable reward power. We cannot tell from the information provided in the case, but there may have been an explicit or implicit offer to provide Jack with some type of tangible benefit in exchange for selecting Standard's software package.

3. What could Mary have done to gain more influence over the decision?

This case points out once again the importance of developing a network of contacts with important people in the organization and outside of it. If Mary had a good relationship with some members of the board, she could have talked to them to make sure they knew about her investigation and her conclusions. Even without this type of network relationship, she may have been able to prevent Jack from distorting her conclusions by sending a copy of the report (or the executive summary) to each board member at the same time she gave it to Jack (telling him that she assumed he would want them to have it in time to prepare for their meeting). This overt tactic is risky, however, because it may engender Jack's hostility and jeopardize her future career at Restview Hospital. Another, more indirect tactic that Mary could have used was to encourage the president of the company with the best software package to lobby directly with board members rather than relying on Jack to present their case. This tactic would be easier to use if she had a good relationship with one or more of the top executives in that company and could rely on their discretion to keep her role in the matter confidential.

It is unlikely that Mary would take any action to influence the decision unless she suspected that Jack would try to distort her recommendations. Depending on how Jack acted in the past, it may not have been evident to her that he would be so biased and deceptive. However, there were some obvious clues such as his insistence that Standard be added to the list of finalists and his lack of interest in the presentations by the other vendors. Perhaps Mary was naive about the politics in the organization and too trustful that Jack would act in the best interest of the organization.

Globe Distributors

The purpose of this case is to develop more skill in analyzing power relations and to gain a better understanding of the way subordinate counterpower may be used against a manager. This is a dramatic example of counterpower, because the subordinates were able to get their boss dismissed for incompetence. Students should read the case and answer the questions on it by themselves, either in class or as homework. After the case is analyzed, it should be discussed in class or in small groups. The discussion requires about 20 minutes.

1. How much power did Norman have over the shipping workers?

Norman has a moderate amount of position power over his subordinates. He has the authority to assign work, and this authority can be used to reward some subordinates with favorable assignments and punish others with unfavorable assignments. He also has the authority to tell subordinates how to do the work. Norman has little authority over basic pay rates, because they are established by the contract negotiated by higher management with the labor union. However, he has the authority to determine which workers may earn extra compensation for working overtime, and this authority is a source of reward power over subordinates. Norman has very limited coercive power, because it is very difficult to dismiss incompetent workers (due to union opposition).

Norman has very little personal power over subordinates except for two cronies who are favored by special treatment. He lacks referent power because most subordinates dislike and distrust him. He lacks expert power because most subordinates do not respect him. They understand that his decisions are guided mostly by concern for his own personal career rather than by concern for the needs of the task and the organization. With regard to Norman's task expertise, it is not clear whether he knows what must be done to improve the performance of his department, but it seems doubtful. Norman's strategy for improving his reputation with superiors is to gain support from sales representatives by accepting special orders and rush orders directly from them. Norman does not seem to realize that this strategy undermines the formal procedures for prioritizing orders, and when carried to extremes it lowers department performance by causing confusion and disrupting normal operations.

2. What counterpower did the workers have over Norman?

The subordinates had little personal power over Norman, because he did not respect their task expertise, and except for his two cronies, he did not care about their friendship. Subordinates had some counterpower due to Norman's dependence on them to get the work done effectively. As in most jobs where there is high formalization, elaborate rules and procedures are not sufficient to ensure high performance by the department. High performance requires some additional direction and coordination by the leader and some initiative and extra effort by subordinates. Performance will suffer when subordinates do the work exactly as specified in formal rules and they fail to take any initiative to solve problems not covered by the rules. With the enthusiastic cooperation of his subordinates, Norman could have had a high performing department that would enhance his reputation with higher management. However, Norman did not appreciate the potential contributions of subordinates to his attainment of desired rewards.

Norman also underestimated the power of subordinates to undermine a manager's reputation by work slowdowns and frequent complaints to higher management. This counterpower could not be used successfully in the past, because Norman was able to persuade higher management that complaints and performance problems were due to worker laziness and incompetence. The vacation period provided a unique opportunity for the workers to demonstrate that they could perform more effectively when Norman was gone than when he was present. In doing so they undermined Norman's credibility with his boss and revealed his incompetence as a manager.

3. Why was Norman unsuccessful in influencing worker motivation?

Norman tried to motivate the workers with intimidation and fear, but they knew that he lacked sufficient position power to force them to work faster and more efficiently. Appeals to their loyalty to the organization or concern for customers would not work, because the workers knew he did not care about anything except his own reputation and career. Performing at the minimal level was a way to express their hatred of Norman, and any intrinsic motivation to achieve excellence was not strong enough to overcome this hatred.

Sporting Goods Store

The purpose of this case is to develop a better understanding of the different types of influence tactics. Another objective is to develop skill in analyzing power relations and planning influence strategies. The exercise requires students to analyze a short case, identify the power sources available to the leader, and estimate the likely outcomes for using various influence tactics in that situation.

Students should read the case prior to class and answer the questions on it by themselves. After the case is analyzed, it should be discussed in class or in small groups. The discussion requires about 30 minutes.

It is best to discuss the power sources before asking students to identify potential influence tactics and the likelihood of success for each one. The information summarizing the manager's power and potential influence tactics can be posted on the blackboard or on a flipchart. Then discuss the best approach for the manager to use, including a combination of tactics used at the same time, or a sequential strategy (e.g., try one influence tactic first, then if it doesn't work, try another one).

1. How much of each type of power does Bill have at this time?

• Legitimate power. Bill has authority to ask an employee to stop wasting time and provide faster service. However, as a new manager with little expertise, subordinates may not perceive the manager to have much authority to prescribe how to do their jobs better, especially when profits for the ski department are already at a level that is average for stores in the region. Thus, Bill has only moderate legitimate power.

• Expert power. Bill has very little relevant expertise. He does not come to the job with an established reputation as an effective manager, which would enhance his expertise in the eyes of subordinates. Instead, he has no prior experience as a store manager, and his limited experience as an assistant manager did not allow him to demonstrate that he knows how to improve profits or satisfy customers. Finally, Bill doesn't ski and knows nothing about skiing.

• Referent power. Bill has just met his subordinates and has not had enough time to establish a deeper relationship with them to provide the basis for referent power. Thus, he has almost zero referent power.

• Reward power. Bill has a limited amount of control over rewards desired by subordinates. He can influence merit pay decisions, but the annual appraisals will not occur for some time and they must reflect objective performance data. Until Bill has actually demonstrated a willingness to reward good performance, his credibility as a source of rewards will not be established with subordinates.

• Coercive power. Bill can fire or suspend employees, but only with the approval of his boss and only by making a strong case. Store profits are not low enough to provide a strong mandate from higher management to "clean up and turn around" the store. Any excessive use of warnings and punishment by a new, inexperienced manager is likely to reflect poorly upon the manager. It will make subordinates unhappy and is likely to increase absenteeism and turnover, thereby undermining any potential gains in profits. Thus, coercive power is very limited in this situation.

2. What influence tactics could be used in this situation to influence Sally? Explain what you would actually say to Sally in the process of using these tactics.

• Simple requests and legitimating tactics. Bill could ask Sally to spend less of her time visiting with customers and more time serving them. Alternatively, he could ask Sally as a department manager responsible for the customer service in her department to reduce waiting time for customers, without mentioning her own contribution to the problem. A store manager has the authority to make these types of requests, and legitimating tactics are probably not needed. When asking Sally to improve customer service, Bill might find it useful to jointly set some specific goals for improved service.

• Rational persuasion. Bill could tell Sally about his observations of dissatisfied customers and explain how faster service will improve department sales and profits.

• Exchange tactics. Bill could promise to recommend a good merit increase if Sally is able to improve customer service in her department and reduce waiting time.

• Personal appeals. Bill has no referent power on which to base a personal appeal, and this tactic is unlikely to be effective.

• Ingratiation. This tactic is likely to improve relationships if it appears to be sincere. For example, he could compliment Sally on her expertise about ski equipment and apparel. However, the potential for using this tactic to get Sally to change her behavior is limited. If Bill compliments Sally then asks her to help provide faster service to customers, the compliment is likely to appear very manipulative.

• Consultation. Bill could tell Sally about his observations of disgruntled customers, suggest that there may be a problem with customer service in her department, and ask her for suggestions about how to deal with the problem. Alternatively, he may invite her to participate in the diagnosis of the problem to determine if customer service really is inadequate and to see if there are other ways to improve department profits.

• Inspirational appeals. Bill could tell Sally that he hopes to make this store the best one in the region, and that her department is essential to the success of the effort. He might say that he would like to see her department gain the reputation of being the best place in town for superb equipment and good service. He could say that he is counting on her help and invite her to join him in achieving this vision.

• Pressure tactics. Bill could criticize Sally's behavior, prod her to provide faster service, or warn her that she is risking her merit increase (and her job) if she continues to waste time visiting while customers are waiting.

• Coalition tactics. Bill has little opportunity to use this indirect influence tactic, since he does not know anybody in the store yet with whom he could form a coalition. A coalition with his boss, the regional manager, is possible but not advisable. Bill should be able to manage the store without running to his boss for help on minor problems like this one.

3. Recommend an influence strategy for Bill to improve store performance.

Many students jump to the conclusion (as Bill did) that the problem is Sally's behavior and the solution is to change it. However, Bill is new to the job and he does not have enough information to diagnose the problem. It is possible that spending more time with customers has benefits as well as costs. Conversations with customers may be used to monitor current ski conditions, recent fads in equipment and apparel, and customer reactions to the various types of ski equipment and apparel sold by the store. Extra time spent with customers may be used to learn more about their needs and provide better advice in the selection of equipment. Finally, socializing with customers may be an aspect of the job that makes it attractive to people such as Sally, despite the low pay. Bill needs to investigate these possibilities before discouraging Sally and other salespeople from spending time with customers. Some excesses may need to be curbed, but there are other things that can be done as well to reduce delays (e.g., better planning of employee work schedules to increase coverage during peak times, better procedures for processing sales quickly, better displays of goods to make it easier for customers to find what they want).

The most promising tactic in this situation is probably consultation because this tactic allows Bill to gather information about the nature of the problem, and it also provides a way to gain Sally's cooperation in dealing with the problem. Of course, some skill is needed to use this tactic effectively, and there is no guarantee that it will be successful in every case. Some use of rational persuasion and inspiration may be appropriate also after Bill gains a better understanding of the problem and its causes. If inspiration is used, it may be advisable to involve the entire store in the vision, not just one department.

The case shows how little power some managers have, even over subordinates, and it requires students to think of ways for a manager to influence subordinates despite minimal position and personal power. However, many students tend to think that Bill's job would be much easier if only he had more position power. One way to challenge this assumption is to modify the case so that Bill is the owner of the store and has complete power to fire employees, give pay increases, and introduce incentive programs based on sales and profits. Then ask students to consider how more power is likely to affect Bill's behavior. The answer is that Bill would probably use his power to coerce and manipulate Sally into providing faster service, without first trying to determine the nature of the problem or the reasons for Sally's behavior. This question leads nicely into a discussion of the benefits and pitfalls of having substantial position power.

Norton Manufacturing

The purpose of this case is to develop skill in analyzing power relations and planning influence strategies. As in the preceding case, this one requires students to identify the power sources available to the manager and estimate the likely outcomes for using various influence tactics in that situation. However, this case deals with lateral influence rather than downward influence.

Students should read the case prior to class and answer the questions on it by themselves. After the case is analyzed, it should be discussed in class or in small groups. The discussion requires about 30 minutes.

It is best to discuss the power sources before asking students to identify potential influence tactics and the likelihood of success for each one. The information summarizing the manager's power and potential influence tactics can be posted on the blackboard or on a flipchart. Then discuss the best approach for the manager to use, including a combination of tactics used at the same time, or a sequential strategy (e.g., try one influence tactic first, then if it doesn't work, try another one).

1. How much power of each type does Rick have over Carl?

Rick has considerable referent power over Carl, because they are friends who occasionally play golf together. Rick also has considerable expert power, because he understands the technical specifications of the products and how to satisfy customer needs. Rick has only limited position power in relation to Carl. As peers in different departments, Rick has no direct authority to tell Carl what to do, and his only legitimate power is the right to request cooperation that is necessary to do his job. However, Carl has many duties and Rick cannot insist that he drop everything else in order to finish developing the specifications and testing the samples for the special order. The moderate lateral interdependence of their jobs provides some opportunities for Rick and Carl to exchange favors (or to cause trouble for each other), but mutual dependence in this relationship limits each person's reward and coercive power.

2. How much power of each type does Rick have over Ken?

Rick has less referent power with Ken than with Carl. Rick and Ken are not close friends, and Ken is distrustful of salespeople due to some earlier conflicts with them. Rick also has less expert power with Ken, because he lacks a detailed understanding of production processes and the problems faced by Ken. As with Carl, Rick has no direct authority to tell Ken what to do, but he has the right to make requests necessary to do his job. However, getting cooperation from Ken will be more difficult, because Rick's request will cause considerable inconvenience and delays for Ken. Although there is some lateral interdependence, it is not symmetrical. Rick is more dependent on Ken than Ken is on Rick, and he does not have much opportunity to provide favors to Ken or to cause him trouble. Thus, Rick's reward and coercive power over Ken is even less than over Carl.

3. What influence tactics would be most effective for influencing Carl to speed up the testing? What would you say to Carl?

The most effective tactic for Rick to use with Carl is probably rational persuasion. Rick can point out how important the order is to the company and how much Carl could contribute to its successful completion. Rick could make a personal appeal to Carl by pointing out that it is important for his career to fill this order successfully (if that is indeed the case). Rick could use exchange tactics by offering a favor or benefit to Carl in return for carrying out the request. Another form of exchange would be for Rick to offer to help Carl do the work on the specifications and tests, thereby making the request easier to fulfill. Ingratiation would only be relevant if Rick stated that Carl is especially qualified to test the samples. For example, Rick could say that Carl is the only one in the company who can do it, or that Carl is the most qualified person to do it. Rick could use consultation by asking Carl if there is anything he could do to speed up delivery of the order, but since it is very obvious what Rick needs Carl to do, the effectiveness of consultation may be limited.

The feasibility of using inspirational appeals is uncertain, because it is not clear in the case whether there is some basis for linking the order to Carl's values, ideals, and self concept. Pressure, legitimating tactics, and coalition tactics are of little relevance in this situation, because they are not justified and would undermine the cooperative relationship Rick has with Carl.

4. What influence tactics would be most effective for influencing Ken to change his production schedule and expedite the special order? What would you say to Ken?

It is less obvious how the various tactics would fare if used to influence Ken to change his production schedule. Rational persuasion may be effective if Rick can show that the benefits from shifting production to the special order will greatly outweigh the benefits of finishing the current run on the regular product. However, the success of such an appeal depends on whether Ken is concerned about company profits, not just about his own immediate production goals. Another potential benefit is that the new customer may bring in enough business to justify purchasing the machines Ken wants. In making his persuasive appeal, Rick must be very diplomatic and sensitive to Ken's concerns. It may be beneficial for Rick to bring a finance or accounting person along to the meeting with Ken to help make his case (a coalition tactic).

Consultation is a more subtle approach, and it may be effective if used in the manner of integrative problem solving. For example, Rick would explain his problem to Ken, and the two managers would mutually explore ideas about the best way to accomplish both their concerns. However, Ken's distrust of salespeople may make it difficult to use this approach.

Personal appeals are not appropriate in this situation, because Rich has no referent power with Ken. Any attempt to use ingratiation would likely appear insincere and manipulative. As with Carl, the feasibility of using inspirational appeals is uncertain, because it is not clear in the case whether there is some basis for linking the request to Ken's values, ideals, and self concept. The possibility of using exchange tactics is limited, because it is not evident that Rich has anything important to offer Ken for his cooperation.

If Ken resists changing his production schedule, Rick could appeal to higher management (another coalition tactic) to resolve the conflict. This tactic is likely to be successful in forcing compliance, but the longer-term costs may outweigh the immediate benefits. Forcing Ken to comply is likely to generate hostility and more distrust, thereby making it difficult to establish a cooperative working relationship in the future. A similar limitation applies to most forms of pressure and legitimating tactics.

National Products

The purpose of this exercise is to develop a better understanding of the implications of different motive patterns for managerial effectiveness. The exercise requires students to analyze a short case, identify the dominant motive pattern of three candidates for general manager, and evaluate their likely effectiveness in this position. Students should read the case and answer the questions on it by themselves, either in class or as homework. After the case is analyzed, it should be discussed in class or in small groups. The discussion requires about 20 minutes.

1. What are the dominant motives for each candidate?

• Charley Adam's dominant needs are esteem and affiliation.

• Bill Stuart's dominant needs are achievement and independence.

• Ray Johnson has a personalized power orientation with strong needs for power, esteem, and security.

2. What are the implications of these traits for the success of each candidate if selected for the general manager position?

Most of the research on managerial motivation suggests that effective managers in large organizations are likely to have a socialized power motive (high need for power combined with emotional maturity), a moderately high need for achievement, and a relatively lower need for affiliation. None of the managers described in this case has the optimal motive pattern for someone who is a general manager in a large organization.

• Charley Adams would tend to emphasize harmonious relationships too much in relation to task objectives; he would avoid making controversial decisions that would put a strain on friendships (e.g., asking subordinates to do extra work or make sacrifices necessary to achieve high performance).

• Bill Stuart would tend to take too much personal responsibility for accomplishing the important and challenging tasks of the group and would not delegate enough or spend enough time developing subordinates.

• Ray Johnson would be domineering and insensitive with subordinates and would probably fail to develop cooperation, trust, and teamwork with them or with peers.

A related supplementary question is whether there is any situation in which the three managers may be more effective, given their motive patterns.

• Charley Adams would probably be most effective as leader who is responsible only for coordinating activities, facilitating teamwork, and making minor decisions for a team of highly-motivated professionals.

• Bill Stuart would probably be most effective in a position where he initiates new projects like an independent entrepreneur, working mostly alone or with a small group of subordinates who are technicians with no aspirations to assume more responsibility.

• Ray Johnson would probably be most effective as the turnaround manager of a bloated, inefficient, possibly corrupt organization that is rapidly failing but is resisting necessary reforms and downsizing. However, to be successful Johnson must have the expertise to know what needs to be done to turn the organization around.

3. Should Susan recommend one of these candidates for the position or look for external candidates?

Susan should look for external candidates. As noted earlier, none of the three internal candidates has the motive pattern usually associated with effectiveness as a middle manager in a large organization. It is also important for a general manager to have knowledge and appreciation of different functional areas in the organization. There is little evidence that the three internal candidates have much expertise outside of their area of functional specialization.

The Intolerable Boss

The purpose of this exercise is to develop a better understanding of the traits that cause people to derail in their managerial careers. The case also provides insights into the emotional stress caused for subordinates by a manager who is arrogant and insensitive. Students should read the case and answer the questions on it by themselves, either in class or as homework. After the case is analyzed, it should be discussed in class or in small groups. The discussion requires about 20 minutes. If some of the students in the class have extensive work experience, it may be useful during the discussion to ask for volunteers to describe their own experiences with an intolerable boss.

1. What traits caused the boss to experience initial career success but eventual derailment?

Qualities of the boss that aided his early career success include incredible technical expertise and the ability to be charming and pleasant to people whom he wanted to impress. These positive qualities were outweighed by some fatal flaws. The boss displayed the typical pattern of arrogance and insensitivity to others that is so common among people who derail in their managerial career. The extreme mood shifts and loss of temper are indicative of low emotional stability. Indicators of low emotional maturity include attacking good ideas rather than encouraging them, making subordinates look stupid, demeaning subordinates in front of others, and rejection of subordinates who make a mistake, regardless of their prior success and overall competence.

2. How difficult is it for someone in Bob's situation to learn useful lessons from experience?

Someone who has an intolerant boss and is experiencing extreme stress and frustration is usually not thinking about opportunities to learn something useful from the experience. It is especially helpful in this situation to have a social support network of people who will provide encouragement and counseling to help the victim survive the experience and learn useful lessons from it. It is also helpful to prepare managers early to expect that sooner or later they are likely to experience various types of adversity, such as an intolerant boss, an incompetent subordinate, political power struggles, hidden problems inherited from a predecessor, assignments for which they lack the necessary expertise, and unfavorable business conditions that undermine the best laid plans.

3. What traits helped Bob survive and learn from his ordeal?

Bob's strong commitment to the organization and his sense of responsibility helped him to focus on doing his job to the best of his ability, rather than dwelling on his career problems and feeling sorry for himself. He had sufficient emotional stability and stress tolerance to keep his composure rather than telling off his boss or quitting in a fit of anger. He was able to detach himself enough from the situation to closely observe the intolerant and demeaning behavior of his boss and make it a lesson in how not to treat people. He was smart enough to find ways to work around the constraints posed by his boss and adapt his behavior to the immediate situation. Finally, he was sufficiently extroverted and sociable to develop a network of colleagues who mutually supported each other, in contrast to someone who is socially isolated and withdrawn.

Precision Plastics

The purpose of this case is to help students gain a better understanding of situational leadership. The case describes a person who appeared to be successful in his initial managerial position but not in a subsequent managerial position. Students are asked to analyze each situation and determine what pattern of managerial behavior is appropriate for it. The analysis gives students an opportunity to develop greater understanding of the importance of adapting one's leadership behavior to the situation.

Students should read the case in class or as homework and answer the questions on it by themselves. After the case is analyzed, it should be discussed in class or in small groups. The discussion requires about 20 minutes.

1. What management style is appropriate in the tool and die department? Refer to any contingency theories of leadership that are relevant for making this analysis.

The task is complex and unstructured, and it requires considerable technical skill to be performed by the workers. The work is very satisfying, however, and it is not very stressful. Joe Casey gives the workers substantial autonomy in determining work procedures and evaluating the quality of the work. It is not clear how much supporting behavior Casey uses with his subordinates, but it is probably not more than a moderate amount.

This pattern of directive and supportive behavior appears to be appropriate according to three of the contingency theories reviewed in Chapter 10. According to path-goal theory, directive, structuring behavior is appropriate when the task is unstructured and workers lack relevant skill and experience, but little directive behavior is necessary when workers are craftsmen or professionals, like the tool and die workers. Supportive behavior is helpful when the task is tedious and stressful, but little supporting is necessary when the work is interesting and enjoyable, as is the case for the tool and die workers.

According to leadership substitutes theory, the experience and intrinsic motivation of the workers serves as a substitute for directive leadership. The intrinsically satisfying task and the companionship of coworkers in the same profession serves as a substitute for supportive leadership. Thus, the supervisor does not need to exhibit high amounts of either type of behavior.

According to the multiple linkage model, considerable delegation of responsibility for work procedures and quality control is appropriate in this situation, because the tool and die makers are competent and highly motivated. However, the model reminds us that other aspects of managerial behavior may be important in this situation (e.g., clarifying priorities, obtaining necessary supplies and materials, coordinating the work with the other departments, and helping to resolve any conflicts).

2. Describe Bill's management style in the molding department and evaluate whether it was appropriate for the situation.

The work of the molding department was routine and highly structured, and it required little skill. According to Bill, the workers have little interest in the work or loyalty to the company. Bill is very task-oriented in his managerial behavior. He directs and supervises the work closely, pushes for higher productivity, and quickly solves production problems. There is no evidence in the case that Bill is supportive toward the workers, and it is likely that he is low on relationship-oriented behavior.

Bill appears to be fairly successful as a supervisor in the molding department; productivity is high and production is usually on schedule. However, there is not much information on how satisfied the molding workers are with their supervisor. The high turnover may be due to the low pay, but it may also reflect worker dissatisfaction with Bill. It is not clear in the case that Bill is correct in his assessment of the workers as lazy and indifferent. He may have created a self-fulfilling prophecy in which the workers are merely acting the way he expects. It is possible that a supervisor with a more balanced concern for task and people would have even higher productivity together with low turnover.

3. Why was Bill unsuccessful in managing the tool and die department?

Bill's management style is not appropriate for the situation. He used close, directive supervision with competent, highly motivated workers who had substantial autonomy under their previous supervisor. In his zeal to organize the department and make it more efficient, Bill attempted to establish rigid rules and procedures for a task that is not susceptible to this type of standardization and formalization. It is a threat to the worker's self esteem and their fulfillment of basic needs and values. Even if it were possible to identify some standard

51

procedures to improve efficiency or quality, Bill lacked the expertise to do it alone. He had no prior experience with this type of task, and he moved quickly to impose changes rather than waiting until he had an opportunity to learn more about the task. Bill's decisions about new work procedures and rules were made in an autocratic manner, rather than consulting with the workers who had extensive expertise about the task. Perhaps Bill assumed that the tool and die workers, like the molding workers, were lazy and indifferent.

It might be possible to make some improvements in efficiency and quality, but Bill is not going about it the right way. In this situation, a combination of participative and inspirational leadership is more likely to result in significant improvements in department performance without undermining worker satisfaction (this type of leadership is discussed in Chapters 11 and 12).

4. What should Jim do now?

Jim needs to recognize that he made a mistake in assigning Bill to supervise the tool and die department without first determining whether there was a good match between Bill's attributes and the requirements of the new leadership situation. Bill's management style is fairly ingrained, and he is not flexible in adapting to different situations. Nevertheless, Jim should make the effort to develop Bill's leadership skills and help him learn more appropriate managerial behaviors. A combination of formal training and individualized coaching is appropriate, but there is no guarantee of success. If Bill is unwilling or unable to change, it may be necessary to transfer him back to the molding department, transfer him to another department with a structured task, or dismiss him.

Foreign Auto Shop

This two-part case gives students an opportunity to develop greater understanding of the importance of flexible leadership in changing situations. Part 1 describes a normal situation and Part 2 describes an unusual crisis situation. Students analyze each situation and determine what pattern of managerial behavior is appropriate. The case illustrates how effective leaders adapt their behavior to the changing requirements of the situation but continue to show concern both for task objectives and interpersonal relationships. The case also demonstrates that an effective leader need not be a "heroic figure" who knows everything and single-handedly solves all of the organization's problems.

Students should read Part 1 and answer the questions on it by themselves; then they should read Part 2 and answer the questions on it. (all prior to class). After the case is analyzed, it should be discussed in class or in small groups. The discussion requires 30 to 40 minutes.

Answers for Part 1

1. What leadership behaviors are appropriate in Alan's situation (consider the nature of the task, subordinates, and environment)?

The repair tasks are mostly self contained, and little coordination is needed between mechanics. Thus, little planning is needed except to determine the work schedule, assignments, and necessary supplies. Except for diagnosis and troubleshooting, most of the repair work is highly structured (there is a best way to do it). However, the tasks require considerable skill, and auto mechanics need to acquire new technical knowledge periodically to keep up with changes in car design and technology. Most of the mechanics in Alan's shop are highly skilled in their work and have considerable experience. The three least experienced mechanics are assigned easier tasks appropriate for their skill level. Although they receive more guidance than the others, even they do not need much supervision. None of the mechanics is younger than twenty-three. They are all highly motivated and interested in their work. Diagnosing auto problems in foreign cars and repairing them is a challenging, self-contained task with moderate variety, and high feedback about results from the task itself and from customers. Thus, except for some routine tasks such as mounting tires and changing the oil, most of the work is intrinsically motivating and satisfying for them.

2. Describe Alan's typical leadership style and evaluate whether it is appropriate for the leadership situation.

Alan's behavior pattern is highly appropriate for his situation. He is a highly participative leader who usually consults with subordinates in making decisions that affect them. He uses general supervision rather than close supervision. That is, he does not spend much time directing subordinates, or checking on their performance. He makes assignments and provides coaching in a casual, non-threatening manner. He does not rely much on the authority stemming from his position as owner and manager of the business. Working along side of the mechanics, he is viewed by them as "one of the crew" rather than as "the boss."

Answers for Part 2

1. Describe Alan's leadership style during the flood and evaluate whether this behavior is appropriate for the leadership situation.

Alan's leadership behavior is appropriate for the situation. By monitoring the external environment, he correctly identifies the flood danger and the need for immediate action by the group to prepare for it. The mechanics have never experienced a flood in the shop, and they have never rehearsed a coordinated response to this type of problem. The flash flood creates a crisis situation, and the mechanics do not know how to respond in a coordinated, effective manner. Thus, quick, decisive problem solving and firm direction are needed to prepare for the flood and coordinate the response of the group. There is no time for participative planning. If the group sat around discussing how to respond, they would not have time to do what is necessary to avoid serious damage to the shop and customer cars.

The situation is complicated by the fact that the mechanics do not recognize the danger and do not believe that Alan is serious when he tells them to drop their regular work and start moving things to safe places. They are confused by his behavior because it is so different from his usual leadership style. Once the mechanics eventually recognize the danger, they will be intrinsically motivated to avoid flood damage that would threaten their jobs. However, there is no time to try to persuade them that there is a crisis. When he sees that the mechanics are not responding to his instructions, Alan becomes much more assertive by giving direct, authoritative orders in a command voice, and using appropriate nonverbal behaviors such as direct eye contact and a stern expression. In effect, Alan falls back on his position power (as owner-manager) to influence subordinates. Although he is firm, he does not use threats or insults.

The flood crisis is novel to Alan as well as to the mechanics, and he cannot think of everything himself. Once the mechanics begin following his directions, Alan is receptive to good suggestions about other things that need to be done to avoid damage to the shop or the cars. Thus, while being very directive, he is still not entirely autocratic in deciding how the group should deal with the problem. Even in a crisis, he is a more effective manager by being receptive to good ideas from subordinates.

2. Identify effective behaviors exhibited by Alan after the flood subsided.

The experience of the flood makes it easier for the mechanics to understand the reason for Alan's authoritative, directive behavior, nevertheless, such behavior carries the risk of undermining his collegial relationship with them. Alan's actions after the crisis are appropriate for maintaining a good relationship. He shows his appreciation for the mechanics' efforts by personally thanking them. As a reward for volunteering to stay late to clean up, he gives them all the next morning off. When they return to work the next afternoon, he makes a speech giving them credit for successfully avoiding serious damage from the flood. He gives recognition for each of their contributions, no matter how small. By these actions, Alan helps the mechanics to perceive the crisis as a joint effort in which they all played important part, rather than as a conflict where he was right, they were wrong, and he was the lone hero.

3. How should Alan behave toward his employees in the future?

There is no reason for Alan to change his typical style of leadership in non-crisis situations. Some students mistakenly interpret the final comments as indicating that Alan needs to become more directive. Such a change would undermine his effectiveness. Alan will have more expert power as a result of his successful interpretation of the crisis, and employees are more likely to believe him and carry out his directions immediately in a future crisis.

Carlson's Raiders

The purpose of this case is to help students gain a better understanding of charismatic leadership. The case describes the leadership behavior of a military officer and the influence he had on his battalion during the early part of World War II. This case is longer than previous ones in the book, because it describes a relationship between leader and followers that develops over a period of more than a year. This longitudinal perspective provides important insights into the complex processes in charismatic leadership. Students are asked to use the major theories of charismatic leadership in the chapter to analyze the case and identify charismatic leadership behaviors and their effects on followers.

Students should read the case prior to class and answer the questions on it by themselves. After the case is analyzed, it should be discussed in class or in small groups. The discussion requires about 30 minutes.

1. What charismatic leadership behaviors did Carlson use?

Colonel Carlson used many of the charismatic behaviors described by key theories such as House, Conger and Kanungo, and Shamir, House and Arthur (see Chapter 11).

• He communicated an inspiring vision that appealed to the values and beliefs of followers. Moreover, he communicated high expectations and expressed confidence that they could achieve them. For example, in his initial speech to the men, he described a new type of military unit that was consistent with their democratic ideals. He told them that they would be able to achieve exceptional feats by developing mutual respect, working as a team, and understanding the purpose of their mission.

• He proposed an unconventional strategy that deviated sharply from the military tradition of that time, including informal relationships between officers and enlisted men, the elimination of special privileges for officers, and the use of participative leadership in planning and evaluating operations. He implemented some innovative combat techniques and used new approaches to training for making the battalion more effective. He used an unconventional strategy when he landed his attacking force on a beach with dangerous reefs that was considered by many (including the Japanese) to be too risky for such a landing.

- He used slogans, rituals, ceremonies, and open discussions to emphasize the values central to his vision, establish the unique identity of the Raiders, and build social identification with the battalion.

- He used role modeling by setting an example in his own behavior of the values he proclaimed for the battalion. He shared their hardships during training, and he exemplified the values of Gung Ho in his daily behavior. During the stress and turmoil of combat he remained calm and confident, thereby increasing the confidence of his men in him and in themselves.

- He used unconventional, symbolic behavior to emphasize his values, such as standing in line with the enlisted men to get food, and standing while others rested during the difficult marches in the jungles of Guadalcanal.

- He took personal risks and made self sacrifices to achieve the vision. For example, he endured unnecessary hardships for an officer during training, and he took unnecessary risks during combat.

- A behavior associated more with transforming leadership (discussed in Chapter 13) than with charismatic leadership was his use of appeals to higher ideals and ethics rather than succumbing to the common practice of using stereotypes and prejudice to build hatred of the enemy.

2. What influence did Carlson have on the effectiveness of the Raiders?

From the evidence in the case, it is apparent that the officers and enlisted men of the battalion had a high level of commitment to their mission, and they maintained a high level of morale even under the most difficult situations. It is evident that many of Carlson's followers attributed extraordinary qualities to him and identified with him as a leader. Many of them also internalized the values that were essential for Carlson's vision. The Raiders identified with their unit, gained confidence from their early achievements, and probably had a strong sense of collective self efficacy. Under Carlson's leadership the battalion became a highly skilled, well organized team. The two missions they were assigned were both carried out successfully, despite unfavorable conditions that would have resulted in failure for a less motivated and skilled unit. Unfortunately, there is little information about the extent to which the changes in culture made by Carlson persisted after he was replaced as the leader of his battalion by an officer who did not subscribe to his ideology.

3. What do you think happened to Carlson's military career after his successful mission on Guadalcanal?

In general, Carlson did not appear to be effective in the political aspects of dealing with higher officers. For example, he was not able to influence the navy bureaucracy to provide adequate motors for the boats during the first mission, which almost resulted in a disaster. He aroused opposition among higher level officers who were jealous of his publicity and threatened by his unconventional ideas. After Guadalcanal, Carlson was assigned to a staff position and he would never again command a combat unit. Most of his unconventional practices were discontinued by his immediate successor. Although some other battalions of marines were formed to perform similar types of missions, those units did not adopt most of Carlson's radical ideas, such as informal relations between officers and enlisted men, elimination of special privileges for officers, participative leadership in planning and evaluating missions, emphasis on flexibility and innovation rather than on following conventional military doctrine and bureaucratic rules, and use of ideological forums to discuss the purpose of the war. The case demonstrates the difficulty of sustaining a drastic culture change in one subunit of large, bureaucratic organization. It is ironic that many of Carlson's unconventional ideas are now standard practice in elite, commando-style units of the United States military. It is also interesting to note that Carlson's experiences of emasculation by the bureaucracy are not unique; the same pattern can be found with other charismatic leaders at lower or middle levels in military and civilian organizations who introduced unconventional ideas that were effective but threatening to more powerful administrators (see for example, *Rogue Warrior*, by Richard Marcinko; Pocket Books, 1992).

Astro Airlines

The purpose of this case, like the preceding one, is to help students gain a better understanding of charismatic leadership. However, in this case the charismatic leader is the CEO of a company rather than a relatively lower level military officer. This case is fairly long, because it describes the behavior of the leader over a period of four years. The charismatic leader establishes a new company that has phenomenal success for the first few years, then quickly declines into bankruptcy. Students are asked to analyze the case and identify charismatic leadership behaviors and their beneficial and dysfunctional effects on followers and on the company.

Students should read the case prior to class and answer the questions on it by themselves. After the case is analyzed, it should be discussed in class or in small groups. The discussion requires about 30 minutes.

1. What charismatic leadership behaviors did Burton use?

• He articulated an appealing vision of a new type of company with an emphasis on quality, informality, participative leadership, and self management that would provide a unique and socially-important service to the nation.

• He took advantage of every opportunity to persistently teach and affirm his vision, and he used emotional, symbolic language.

• His vision involved an unconventional strategy of no frills, one-class airline service with innovative scheduling of flights and in-flight ticketing. Other unconventional ideas implemented by Burton included elimination of status perks for executives, required ownership of company stock by employees, extensive use of participation to make some types of decisions, elimination of narrow role specialization, and emphasis on teams to do the work.

• He used symbolic behavior to demonstrate his commitment to key values. For example, he participated in the training of new executives.

2. What dysfunctional aspects of charismatic leadership occurred in this company?

• Burton's strong self confidence and experience of early success may have resulted in overinflated self assessment and over-optimism about his strategic decisions. For example, in pursuit of a grander vision of quickly becoming an international airline (rather than a small regional carrier), he acquired other airlines that were already financially weak, thereby incurring a dangerous amount of debt that would contribute to the failure of the firm. In his plans to expand the number of routes and flights, he ignored the threat of reaction by powerful competitors, and he was overoptimistic about the number of people who would want to use his no-frills service.

• He was too focused on the big-picture aspects of the vision and neglected the details of its implementation. He did not spend the time necessary to identify and resolve serious organizational problems that stemmed in part from rapid growth and in part from some of his beliefs about the best way to organize. At one point he finally acknowledged that there were serious organizational problems and promised to deal with them, but continued to emphasize rapid growth rather than consolidation and refinement of the management systems.

• He became very defensive about his ideas and very autocratic in his decisions, even though his ideology was one of participative leadership. For example, he assumed the responsibilities of the president when that position became vacant, he fired executives who disagreed with him, and he maintained tight control over the board of directors.

• The same optimism and adherence to unconventional strategies that made him appear brilliant and charismatic to employees and investors when the company had unusual early success, made him appear rigid and incompetent when the company went into a sharp decline. In other words, his success with innovative strategies caused attributions about exceptional expertise, but these attributions rapidly changed when success turned to failure.

Southwest Engineering Services

The purpose of this case is to help students gain a better understanding of transformational leadership. The case describes the leadership behavior of a project manager over a period of several months. Students are asked to analyze the case and identify examples of transformational leadership behaviors and their effects on followers. Students should read the case prior to class and answer the questions on it by themselves. After the case is analyzed, it should be discussed in class or in small groups. The discussion requires 20 to 30 minutes.

1. Describe the leadership behaviors Ron used and their influence on the attitudes and behavior of the team members.

Ron developed a highly cohesive team that was strongly committed to the project, and the project was completed successfully ahead of schedule. He used the following pattern of leadership behaviors to accomplish this outcome:

• He talked about developing a leading edge decision support system that will be essential for the company to remain profitable, and this vision appealed to the values and needs of the systems engineers.

• He set a challenging objective for them and expressed confidence that they could achieve it if there was total commitment by every member.

• He told the engineers that they were all especially qualified to work on this important project, which probably increased their self worth and sense of individual and collective self efficacy.

• He explained how difficult and intense the work would be and asked each individual to decide whether or not to join the team. The ritual of openly acknowledging allegiance to the project probably helped to strengthen commitment to the project and identification with the team.

• He had an attitude of enthusiasm and optimism that spread to the team members and helped them have confidence in Ron and themselves. For example, when the team became discouraged about lack of progress, he gave them a pep talk to boost their optimism and enthusiasm.

• He achieved a good balance between directing and empowering, which was appropriate for the situation. He communicated a clear picture of the specifications necessary for the new system, thereby clarifying what they had to accomplish and keeping them focused on the same objective. At the same time, he delegated considerable responsibility to individuals and gave them discretion to determine how their work should be accomplished.

• He used participative leadership extensively, which was appropriate for the type of task and subordinates. Frequent team meetings were held to collectively evaluate their progress and decide how to deal with obstacles and problems. Influence over these decisions depended on expertise and quality of ideas, not status or years in the company.

• He achieved a good balance of task and person orientation. He was supportive and helpful when someone was experiencing difficulties, and he took time to develop and mentor subordinates, giving them opportunities to develop new skills and encouraging them to consider more ambitious career objectives. At the same time, he pushed relentlessly for continued progress in the work and made it clear that he would not tolerate less than a maximum effort.

• He used his network of political relationships to obtain necessary resources and cooperation from peers and superiors.

2. Use the leadership theories in Chapters 11 and 12 to analyze the case and determine whether Ron should be classified as a charismatic leader, a transformational leader, or both.

Ron can be regarded as a transformational leader. He inspired and empowered subordinates, who made an exceptional effort, put the needs of the project above their individual needs, and achieved more than they initially expected. It is clear that Ron was highly liked and respected by the team members, but they perceived the achievements of the team as the result of a collective effort. Conger and Kanungo's theory would explain the lack of attributed charisma in the following way: Ron did not develop an unconventional vision or strategy, he did not engage in unconventional behavior, he did not make great personal sacrifices to accomplish the project, he did not demonstrate extraordinary task expertise, and there was no immediate crisis.

Metro Bank

The purpose of this case, like the preceding one, is to help students gain a better understanding of transformational leadership. The case describes the leadership behavior of a bank manager over a period of several months. Students are asked to analyze the case and identify examples of transformational leadership behaviors and their effects on followers. Students should read the case prior to class and answer the questions on it by themselves. After the case is analyzed, it should be discussed in class or in small groups. The discussion requires about 20 to 30 minutes.

1. What leadership behaviors did Marsha use to change the branch office and motivate employees?

Marsha transformed a branch bank with low morale, efficiency, and customer service to one with high morale, efficiency, and customer service. She used the following pattern of leadership behaviors to accomplish this outcome:

• Marsha formulated a vision to give her branch bank (one of many) a distinctive character and a clear mission. This vision was formulated only after she had been in her new position for a few months and got to know her employees, the situation at the branch, and the politics of corporate headquarters.

• Her vision involved the two strategic objectives of developing executive talent and providing quality customer service, and she looked for ways to integrate these objectives so that they would be mutually facilitative.

• Her vision and strategy were communicated through her statements, decisions, and day-to-day actions. She declared that opportunities for development would be available to all employees, not just to fast-track managers, and she followed up on her promise by negotiating access to the management development program for any employees who aspired to advance into higher level management.

• She used developmental assignments and coaching to increase the managerial skills of her immediate subordinates.

- She instituted a number of organizational changes, including cross training to increase employee skills as well as customer service, and modification of the appraisal/reward system to provide tangible benefits to employees who helped others learn.

2. Use the leadership theories in Chapters 11 and 12 to analyze the case and determine whether Marsha should be classified as a charismatic leader, a transformational leader, or both.

Marsha can be regarded as a transformational leader in the sense that she both inspired and empowered subordinates to achieve more than they initially expected. The bank employees came to see their work roles as crucial for individual and organizational success rather than as a thankless task. Employees felt increased pride in their work and internalized the values of helping others learn and providing quality service to customers. Some old-timers acquired new aspirations and advanced to higher positions.

However, employees did not appear to view Marsha as a charismatic leader. Once again, there is little evidence of the types of behaviors necessary (according to Conger and Kanungo) for attributed charisma. She did not propose an unconventional vision and strategy. The objectives for the branch already included executive development and customer service. What Marsha did was to make these objectives more meaningful and relevant for regular bank employees. She increased both the ideological significance of the developmental objective for employees and the tangible benefits for helping to make the program successful. She did not engage in unconventional behavior or make significant personal sacrifices to achieve her vision. Although Marsha was put in charge of a branch with some discontented employees and lower than expected performance, there was no serious crisis requiring unconventional strategies and actions. Finally, although Marsha demonstrated considerable competence as a manager in turning around her branch, she did not display exceptional genius in solving highly visible problems that are central to the survival and success of the organization (e.g., she did not introduce successful new products or services, bring in important new customers, or defeat competitors who threatened to ruin the bank).

Falcon Computer Company

The purpose of this case is to help students gain a better understanding of the effects of leaders on organizational culture. The case describes an organization in which top management attempted to change the culture. Students are asked to analyze the case and explain why the attempted culture change was unsuccessful. Students should read the case in class or as homework and answer the questions on it by themselves. After the case is analyzed, it should be discussed in class or in small groups. The discussion requires about 20 to 30 minutes.

1. Why was the actual culture so discrepant from the written document?

Use of a written values statement has little effect on the actual culture of an organization if not supported by other mechanisms for changing and maintaining culture. The values statement represented the espoused values of the organization, which were not consistent with the underlying values and beliefs of organization members. In dealing with problems of external adjustment and internal integration, top management acted in ways that exemplified values inconsistent with the values statement.

For example, the values statement advocated open, two-way communication as a key value governing internal relations among members of the organization, but top management dominated meetings and discouraged suggestions or criticisms from employees. It was a highly symbolic action when top management created the values document in secret without any input from other managers and employees. This incident became the subject of a story that circulated among employees and served to undermine the espoused value.

The values document advocated delivery of defect free products on time as a key value governing relationships with customers, but the daily behavior of top management emphasized the primary importance of quick delivery, and employees were actually discouraged from pointing out defects. Rather than acting in ways to strengthen the espoused values, some members of management acted in ways that undermined them.

2. What could have been done by the top executives to make the culture of the organization more consistent with the values statement? Describe specific actions to embed the values of open communication and exceptional product quality in the culture.

The types of leadership actions necessary to build a strong culture are described in Chapter 12. Leaders communicate their priorities and values by what they ask about, measure, comment on, praise, and criticize in their day-to day behavior. A strong message about values and priorities is communicated also by the allocation of rewards and the criteria used for selection, promotion, and dismissal. The organization structure and management systems should be designed in a way that is consistent with key objectives and values. Finally, oral and written statements of values are useful if they are consistent with the other mechanisms for influencing culture.

The following actions could be taken by top management to embed open communication as a key value in the culture:

•   Provide more opportunities for all employees to communicate openly with top management (informal meetings, special times when employees can drop in to see top management without an appointment, hot lines, more management by walking around).

•   Eliminate obvious status symbols and communication barriers such as separate dining rooms and other facilities for top management.

•   Share more information with employees about the performance of the company and top management activities.

•   Encourage questions and expression of suggestions and concerns.

•   Show appreciation for ideas and suggestions.

•   Make a serious effort to use suggestions and deal with concerns.

•   Don't punish people who criticize weaknesses in plans or policies, or who point out problems that need to be addressed.

The following actions could be taken by top management to embed exceptional product quality as a key value in the culture:

• Articulate a clear vision in which quality is a key value.

• Involve people at all levels in a program for the continuous improvement of quality.

• Create new structural mechanisms such as quality circles and empower them to take necessary actions to resolve quality problems.

• Talk about quality, ask questions about it, and review quality indicators frequently in daily behavior.

• Develop better internal systems and procedures for measuring quality and identifying quality problems.

• Devote more resources to discovering customer preferences and monitoring of customer reactions to the firm's products.

• Recognize and celebrate contributions to quality improvement made by individuals and teams.

• Include responsibility for quality as a performance dimension in all management and nonmanagement jobs.

• Make quality a primary criterion for rewarding employees.

• Use criteria relevant to quality in selecting and promoting employees.

Northstar Corporation

The purpose of this case is to help students gain a better understanding of strategic leadership by top executives. The case describes a company that is experiencing declining sales and profits following a long period of prosperity. Students are asked to analyze the case and determine what should be done to revitalize the company. Students should read the case prior to class and answer the questions on it by themselves. After the case is analyzed, it should be discussed in class or in small groups. The discussion requires about 20 to 30 minutes.

1. What specific types of actions by top management are needed to revitalize this company?

The strategy of selling highly-priced products for which the company is the exclusive supplier is no longer feasible. Conditions in the environment have changed, and the company now has new competitors who are challenging its dominance of the market. The company needs to develop new products, improve product quality, strengthen its marketing, and reduce its overhead costs by downsizing. Strategic changes of this magnitude require supporting changes in the culture of the organization. For example, relevant values (e.g., exceptional quality, product and process innovation, continuous improvement, and teamwork) must be strengthened.

The chief executive needs to identify a new strategy appropriate for the organization and its environment, articulate a vision that embodies the core values, and build a broad coalition to provide political support for implementing the new strategy. It is likely that changes in the top management team will be necessary, including replacement of some executives who are unable to accept the new strategy. Supporting changes in the organization structure are needed also. Some structural changes that may be appropriate include creation of a strong marketing group and a strong product development group, use of more cross-functional teams to facilitate development of innovative new products with high quality, and implementation of a reward system that supports the new values. Downsizing will probably require elimination of unnecessary layers of middle management and useless administrative staff.

2. How likely is it that Henry will try to make drastic changes in the strategy and culture of the organization?

The research evidence indicates that most chief executives with a long tenure are unable to give up old ways of doing things and make radical changes in the strategy of their organization, even to save it from bankruptcy. Because Henry Miles is the company founder and major architect of the old strategy and culture, it will be difficult for him to make substantial changes. On the other hand, with an obvious crisis it is difficult for Henry to deny the need for major adjustments in strategy. The answer will depend greatly on what type of person Henry Miles really is, including his personality, values, and leadership skills. Henry is more likely to embrace a new strategy if it reflects core values of the company in its earlier days and it allows Henry to preserve the best part of his original creation, rather than renounce it entirely. The core values of the earlier culture are not clear from the case.

3. If an effort is made to change the strategy and culture of the organization, what difficulties and obstacles are likely to be encountered?

Many of the usual obstacles are present, including people who do not want to give up power and status, and people who cling to the old ways and resist any change. With an obvious crisis, the leader is expected to make major changes, and these changes are more likely to be accepted than in a non-crisis situation. However, much will depend on the relative power of different stakeholders. It is not clear from the case whether there are important outside stakeholders such as large stockholders, bankers, and customers that may favor a particular strategy. It is also unclear how much power the various stakeholders have, and how they perceive the crisis. As the company founder and a major stakeholder (it is likely that he still holds a large block of stock), Henry probably has more power than most chief executives to hold onto his job and initiate revitalization of the company. He is more likely to succeed if he can define events in such a way that people do not blame him for the crisis and they perceive that his proposed strategy is feasible.

Building Maintenance Inc.

The purpose of this case is to help students gain a better understanding of leadership in decision groups. The case describes a meeting by the company president and the other top executives to make an important decision for the company. Students are asked to analyze the case and identify effective and ineffective leadership behaviors. Students should read the case prior to class and answer the questions on it by themselves. After the case is analyzed, it should be discussed in class or in small groups. The discussion requires about 20 to 30 minutes.

1. Identify effective and ineffective actions by Bud in conducting the meeting.

Bud exhibited several examples of effective leadership in conducting the group meeting:

• Prior to the meeting he asked Karen to gather information about the cost of the different options and report this information at the meeting.

• He provided a clear and brief statement of the problem.

• He avoided stating his own preferences before hearing from the others.

• He asked each person for ideas and opinions to ensure complete participation.

• He used restatement of Liz's comment to test for understanding and clarify her point.

• He ignored irrelevant comments by Marty about the rude order clerks, rather than letting the discussion get off the track.

• He ignored the irrelevant question by Liz about refreshments.

Bud also exhibited several examples of ineffective leadership in conducting the group meeting:

• He was late to his own meeting (however, he did apologize to the group).

• He initially redefined the problem in terms of a choice between two options, which tends to discourage identification of other options (such as having more than one office).

• He did not intervene to cut off the irrelevant discussion about a company party.

• He gave up too easily on reaching a decision when he found that there was no easy consensus. He should have kept the group working longer on the primary issue, rather than turning to another, less important subject that they were not prepared to discuss.

• He failed to summarize what had been learned about the advantages and disadvantages of the major options, thereby missing an opportunity to end on a positive note by pointing out that something worthwhile was accomplished in the meeting.

• It was not necessary to reach a decision at this meeting, but instead of having people prepare for another meeting on the subject, Bud gave up and decided to hire a relocation consultant. This action communicated a lack of trust in the group to make a relatively easy decision, thereby undermining its confidence about making other, more difficult decisions in the future.

2. What could have been done to make the meeting more successful?

• Bud should have structured the meeting so that alternatives were identified before they were evaluated. For example, he could have used brainstorming or the nominal group method of idea generation. A prolonged effort to identify alternatives may have identified some additional ones, such as the possibility of buying their own building.

• He should have structured the meeting so that after alternatives were generated, the group made a systematic evaluation of the costs and benefits for each alternative. This information is complex, and it could be posted on a flip chart for members of the group to study.

• He should have spent some time identifying the outcomes to be considered in evaluating alternatives. It is likely that this step would have identified some additional factors, such as the difficulty of commuting to each office site (by employees who work in the office), and other expenses besides rent and relocation costs (e.g., local taxes, utilities, parking, cost of transporting equipment to work sites, etc.).

• After various criteria were identified, he should have tested for agreement on the relative priorities of these criteria, especially if the group seemed to be polarized between two competing alternatives. An explicit discussion of different criteria and their priorities also helps to reduce the likelihood that the relocation decision will be determined primarily by implicit criteria that are not even discussed in the meeting, such as the commuting distance for key executives.

• He should have probed with questions to determine if people had any factual evidence to support their opinions about outcomes. For example, Marty claimed that a suburban office would improve the company's image, but he was about to leave for a lunch meeting with a client at a restaurant. It would be useful to determine how often clients actually come to the office and whether they really expect a cleaning and maintenance company to have a plush suburban office. Liz claimed that a downtown office would be necessary to recruit workers and handle personnel matters, but Nick said that most of the workers seldom come to the office after they are hired. It would be useful to determine how often and for what reasons workers come to the office, and whether most of these visits can be handled in other ways (for example, hiring may be done at an employment agency). Karen claimed that the company could not afford two offices, but the basis for this conclusion was not determined (costs would depend on the size and type of facilities; a medium-sized suburban office combined with a very small downtown office may be no more expensive than renting one larger suburban office).

Allied Industries

Like the preceding case, the purpose of this one is to help students gain a better understanding of leadership in decision groups. The case describes a meeting held by a middle manager to determine how to handle an impending problem about which employees have strong feelings and opinions. Students are asked to analyze the case and identify effective and ineffective leadership behaviors. Students should read the case prior to class and answer the questions on it by themselves. After the case is analyzed, it should be discussed in class or in small groups. The discussion requires about 20 to 30 minutes.

1. Identify effective and ineffective behavior by Mark and the other people in the meeting.

Examples of effective behaviors:

• Kim asked Wally to stop casting blame and focus on solving the problem.

• Brian asked Wally for evidence to support his claims that employees were against carpools.

• Mark told Wally that his criticism was inappropriate.

• Brian tried to build on Neil's idea.

• Mark scheduled a followup meeting to continue working on the problem and assigned responsibility to various people (including himself) to gather information needed at that meeting.

• Mark kept encouraging people to generate more ideas about possible solutions.

Examples of ineffective behaviors:

• Wally immediately criticized Mark and top management for not dealing with the issue earlier, which does nothing to help solve the problem.

• Wally made sarcastic remarks to shoot down suggestions by Jane and Neil.

• Mark's assignment to Jane was a little vague ("think about designing a survey on employee attitudes"); it is better to ask her to develop a draft version of a survey to be discussed at the next meeting.

2. What could have been done to make the meeting more successful?

• Mark should have allowed more time than 30 minutes for the meeting, unless it was just an exploratory session limited to generating possible solutions.

• He should have structured the meeting so that promising alternatives were identified before they were evaluated (using brainstorming or the nominal group method of idea generation).

• When it was time to evaluate the alternatives, he should have structured the discussion so that the group made a systematic evaluation of the costs and benefits of each alternative, which could be posted on a flip chart for all to see.

• Knowing that Wally was going to be disruptive, he should have talked to Wally before the meeting in an effort to influence him to be more cooperative and helpful.

• Another option would be to set some standards of behavior at the beginning of the meeting by asking the group not to say anything negative about an idea until after saying something positive, and not to point out weaknesses without suggesting ways to overcome them.

• He could have done more to summarize all of the ideas at the end of the meeting (he did so only indirectly in making assignments).

• He should have given more recognition to the group for coming up with such a good set of ideas in a short period of time.

Role Plays and Other Exercises

General Guidelines on Multiple Role Playing

These guidelines assume that you will use multiple role plays by forming students into small groups and providing a copy of the role play materials to each group. This procedure is feasible if the classroom has movable chairs and there is enough space to set up circles of chairs for groups in different parts of the room. When several groups do a role play at the same time it gets very noisy and there can be considerable confusion unless students understand in advance what they are expected to do. It is helpful to clarify the procedure for students, facilitate the process of forming groups and selecting roles, start all of the groups at the same time, and set clear time limits for ending the role play. The following suggestions will facilitate the use of multiple role plays and make them more successful.

1. Before role plays are used in the class, take the time to explain why they are used and what students are expected to do. Make sure students know that when used properly role plays provide an opportunity for them to build their skills. Remind students that role plays are a serious learning method that is widely used in workshops for executives and managers.

2. Encourage students who are hesitant by saying that the roles do not require special acting skills; anyone in the class is capable of doing them. They should try to have enough emotional involvement to make the role play seem real, but not so much that it becomes more than an experiential exercise. In other words, they should not become defensive, angry, or upset with things said by other students when playing their roles.

3. Encourage students to help each other learn from the exercises rather than being overly critical. Remind students that learning to provide constructive feedback is a skill they need to become effective managers, and this skill can be practiced after each role play, regardless of whether the student is a player or observer. Compliment appropriate supportive and constructive behavior by students after the role plays.

4. When role plays are used for skill practice, it is helpful to have students review relevant behavioral guidelines beforehand. One type of review is to show an overhead summarizing the guidelines. Another approach is to ask volunteers to provide a guideline without looking at the book, and write the guidelines on the board or flipchart until all of them are listed.

5. Have students familiarize themselves with their designated roles beforehand and plan in a general way what they will say. Students should be encouraged to study their role materials and take notes on key facts to be used in the role play.

6. Students should not show their written roles to each other either before or during the role play. During the role plays, students should convey all information orally, and it is more realistic if students do not read from their role descriptions in a mechanical manner.

7. Remind students to play a role the way they think a real employee would react in that situation. It is okay to change one's initial position during the course of the role playing when it is reasonable to expect that a person would do so after being exposed to additional information. Students may add information to embellish the role, but they should not make up substantive facts that change the situation in a significant way.

8. Vary the composition of the groups used for role plays and case discussions rather than keeping the same groups all during the course. Students are exposed to different points of view, and they are more likely to focus on doing the exercise than on socializing or dealing with underlying relationships. It is also helpful to vary role assignments across exercises so that different students get an opportunity to play the role of the key manager.

Description of the Role Play Exercises

The role play exercises included in this manual were selected to provide a sample of the types of role plays relevant for practicing skills in managerial leadership. Because of the limited space in this manual, only four role plays could be included, and they deal with only a small part of the material in the book. The KB Sportswear role play is concerned primarily with managing conflict between two subordinates, and it is most relevant to Chapter 5. The Save Mart role play is concerned primarily with delegating to a subordinate, and it is most relevant to Chapter 6. Union Chemicals and Baxter Manufacturing both involve decision making by a management group, and they allow students to practice the meeting leadership guidelines covered in Chapter 14.

If additional role plays are desired, there are a number of good sources. Structured role plays can be found in many books on management and organizational behavior that include experiential learning exercises. One example of a book with many role plays is *Training in Interpersonal Skills*, by Stephen Robbins (Prentice Hall, 1989). Some of the cases in the leadership book can be used also as the basis for role playing (e.g., Sterling Products, American Financial, Sporting Goods Store, Norton Manufacturing). For people who enjoy case writing, it is not difficult to develop new role plays that are relevant for a particular aspect of leadership and appropriate to the interests of your students. Finally, for evening students who have regular day jobs, it is sometimes useful to have students play roles based on actual incidents in their jobs. This approach is more successful if a student prepares in advance a written description of the incident with sufficient information for other role players to understand the situation.

KB Sportswear Role Play

How to Use the Role Play

The objective of this role play exercise is to give students an opportunity to experience a conflict situation involving management issues. The role play involves a conflict between the Vice President for Sales and the Vice President for Production. The person playing the role of company president has an opportunity to practice third party mediation and process consultation techniques.

For this role play exercise it is necessary to form four-person groups and determine for each group who will play the role of the three executives and who will serve as the observer. Extra students may be assigned as additional observers. After roles are assigned, give students copies of the materials relevant for their part in the role play exercise. Each student should be given a copy of the general instructions and background information. In addition, students selected to be managers should get a copy of their respective roles. Students selected to be observers should get a copy of the instructions for observers, the observer sheet, and the key on ways to reduce causes of the conflict.

Before beginning the role play, students should read the background information and study their roles. Students selected to be observers should study the special instructions for observers and the form for taking notes on the meeting. These notes will be the basis for providing feedback to their group, and especially to the student playing the role of KB President. Remind students not to look at the materials for any other person, either before or during the role play. During the role play, information should be communicated only orally, and students should not show their printed role sheets to each other.

After the role play, reconvene the class to discuss it. Have the observer for each group report how they dealt with the issues. Ask for examples of especially effective behavior by students who played the role of the KB president.

The total time for the exercise is about an hour. It takes about 5 minutes to introduce the exercise, form groups, and distribute copies of the materials. Students need 10 minutes to read their materials and prepare for the role play. Allow about 15 minutes for the role play itself, and another 10 minutes for feedback from the observer. The class discussion takes about 15 minutes.

KB Sportswear

General Instructions for Students

The purpose of this role play is to provide an opportunity for you to experience what it is like to be in a conflict situation involving management issues. The role play involves three parties: the president of KB Sportswear, the Vice President for Sales, and the Vice President for Production. If you are selected to play the role of one of these executives, you will be provided with a description of your role. Before the role play begins, read the background information and study the description of your role. Try to imagine how the person would actually feel in that situation and act accordingly during the role play. Please do not look at the materials for any role other than the one that you are selected to play.

One or more observers will be assigned to each group. If you are selected to be an observer, use the observer form to take notes on how the conflict was handled. These notes will be used to provide feedback to the managers after the role play is completed. Your instructor will provide additional information on procedures and time limits for the role play.

Background Information for KB Sportswear

KB Sportswear is a small company that manufactures clothing used in sports and recreational activities, including ski apparel, jogging outfits, swim wear, tennis outfits, and clothing for hunting and fishing. The company's sportswear is manufactured at two small plants just across the border in Mexico. KB sells its sportswear to a variety of department stores, sporting goods stores, and clothing stores, including small, individually-owned stores as well as large chain stores.

The sportswear markets serviced by the company are increasingly dominated by fads and fashion trends. Items such as ski jackets and jogging outfits are often purchased for general use, not just for use in a sports activity. In any given year, some styles and patterns for a particular type of sportswear are likely to be more popular than others. The stores typically order only a limited quantity of various items, then place followup orders for particular styles that are selling well. Since most sportswear is seasonal and fashions change from year to year, it is very important for stores to receive quick delivery on these reorders. Otherwise, they miss opportunities for profitable sales and may be stuck with inventory that cannot be sold except at greatly reduced prices during post-season sales.

The company has a sales force of twenty sales representatives, each with a different territory. The sales representatives work on a commission basis. Since one basis for making sales is the promise of quick delivery, there is intense pressure from the sales representatives to get a reorder filled quickly. Orders made by the stores are placed with the sales representatives or sent by mail directly to the headquarters sales office in Los Angeles. Reorders are usually called in to the sales office by the sales reps, or by the customers themselves. A credit check is made on the customer by the sales office before an order is sent to the headquarters production office. Depending on the results of a credit check, the customer may be required to pay in advance before an order is filled.

By the time most reorders come in, the plants are usually in the middle of production runs on items for the next season. If this production is disrupted, the line of sportswear for the next season may not be ready on time. During the past two years, average delivery time for reorders has increased from three weeks to six weeks, and relations between sales and manufacturing have deteriorated over this issue. The President has called a meeting with the two vice presidents at company headquarters in Los Angeles to deal with the growing conflict.

KB Sportswear

Role for President

You have been the President of KB Sportswear for the last five years. The company has been growing steadily in sales, and its lines of sportswear are now being sold in most parts of the United States. However, the problem of delivery delays on reorders threatens to cut into sales, and may have done so already. You believe that the company has enough plant capacity to produce all of the sportswear that it can sell this year if the production scheduling problems can be worked out.

There are several constraints on solving the problem. The company cannot afford to maintain large inventories of items if it is going to be stuck with many unpopular lines that do not sell. KB cannot afford to build or buy another plant at the present time, although in another year or two it may be feasible. If absolutely necessary it is possible to subcontract some work to other companies. However, subcontracting production would increase costs, which are now at minimum levels, and would not necessarily guarantee any faster delivery of reorders. You hope that you can help to resolve the conflict between the sales and production vice presidents and get them to cooperate in discovering how to reduce delays in delivery of reorders.

KB Sportswear

Role For VP-Sales

You are glad that this meeting is being held so that you can express your growing frustration with the production people. Don't they understand that without sales there wouldn't be any company? Nearly half of KB's sales are accounted for by reorders. You are proud of your record in increasing sales over the last two years, but the same kind of increase will not be possible in the next two years if there are long delays in deliveries of reorders. Even now, some potential sales are being lost to other companies who guarantee faster delivery. Once a company gets a bad reputation about late deliveries, it becomes difficult to obtain any business from the large stores that are your most important customers.

Several of the sales reps have complained to you that the production people are uncooperative. When the sales reps try to find out about an order, they usually can't get a definite answer. How can they make sales if it is impossible to tell a customer how long it will take to get a reorder? You heard through the grapevine that one of your sales reps stopped in at the plant last week to check on a special order and was told never to come back.

You believe that production is entirely at fault for the problem of slow deliveries on reorders. All they seem to care about is saving a few dollars on production costs. The production scheduling doesn't seem to make any sense. Sometimes a sales rep has to wait six weeks for a reorder, and other times the same type of order is filled in two weeks. Why can't production fill all of the reorders in two or three weeks? You wonder why things are so screwed up in production. Are the managers in those Mexican plants are taking too many siestas?

In addition, your sales reps complain that production doesn't seem to have any sense of priorities. A reorder for a small store is sometimes filled before a reorder for a major customer like a department store chain. If production cannot do all of the reorders quickly, then they should expedite reorders for the major customers and let the less important customers wait longer.

You believe that the production mess can be straightened out with better management. If it is not possible to speed up deliveries with the present facilities, then the company should build another plant or subcontract the reorders to other companies. Most of KB's lines could be made anywhere in the world, such as in Korea or China.

KB Sportswear

Role For VP-Manufacturing

You have been looking forward to this meeting, because it is about time something was done about the sales representatives. All they seem to care about is making fat commissions. They make unrealistic promises of fast delivery to stores, then they expect miracles from production to bail them out. They have become especially obnoxious lately in pestering the plant managers or anybody else they can talk to about reorders. Production people are constantly getting telephone calls from one sales rep or another checking on reorders. Some sales reps attempt to influence a plant manager to give them favorable treatment. You heard that last week one sales rep even came to the plant and offered a bribe for doing his order first. The manager threw him out and told him never to show his face in that plant again!

You are proud that production of sportswear by KB has been increased substantially, while keeping unit costs below the industry average. It is this success that allows the company to remain competitive in its pricing of sportswear. However, you cannot keep production costs down if you have to keep interrupting the high-volume work on next season's lines to make a small batches of reorder items. Why don't the sales reps understand that you can't shut down regular production every time they have some little ski shop in Vermont that wants a dozen ski jackets? If the sales people could tell you sooner which items are selling well, rather than waiting for actual reorders, you could build up larger inventories of the "hot" items.

You are aware that the delivery time on reorders has gotten worse, but it is not your fault. As sales have increased in the last two years, the two plants have come close to full capacity, making the scheduling of production for reorders even more difficult than before. Your plant managers usually delay production on reorders until there is enough volume of a particular type of item to make it economical to interrupt the regular production. Only very large reorders that don't have to be combined with other orders get processed quickly.

Delays in delivery of reorders are due also to the tougher requirements for credit checks instituted last year by the headquarters sales office. Before you can fill a reorder you must wait for a credit check on the customer to be completed, even for major department stores worth many times more than KB Sportswear. Relaxing these requirements would help speed up deliveries on some of the reorders.

KB Sportswear

Instructions For Observer

Your job is to observe the role play and take notes on how well the student playing the role of boss manages the conflict between the two vice presidents. In preparation for the role play, read the background information, the observer form, and the key on possible ways to resolve the problem causing the conflict. The relevant guidelines for managing conflict are listed on the observer form. During the role play, make a checkmark next to any behavior used by the person who plays the role of company president, and write notes describing relevant details of managerial behavior. Use your notes as basis for giving feedback to the leader after the role play is completed.

Observer Form

Problem-Oriented Actions

___1. Encourage each party to describe the conflict in situational terms not personal terms.

___2. Provide factual information relevant to the problem or help verify it.

___3. Encourage each party to disclose their real needs and priorities.

___4. Encourage both parties to identify shared objectives and values.

___5. Encourage generation of integrative solutions after the problem is defined.

___6. Suggest helpful compromises or integrative solutions not obvious to the parties.

___7. Check to ensure commitment of both parties to any agreements.

Relationship-Oriented Actions

____1. Remain impartial and show acceptance and respect toward both parties.

____2. Discourage threats, insults, stereotyping, and exaggerations.

____3. Use humor or smoothing when appropriate to reduce tension.

____4. Ensure each party has opportunity to speak and nobody dominates the conversation.

____5. Ask each party to describe how they view the other's behavior and intentions.

____6. Encourage active listening (e.g., discourage interruptions, ask each party to restate what the other party said).

____7. Have the parties discuss the discrepancy between their own self-perception and the way the other party perceives them.

____8. Ask each party to select one or two things they will change to improve relations.

____9. Plan another meeting to check on progress and continue the process.

Observer Key for KB Sportswear Role Play

What the Sales VP Can Do

• Prohibit sales reps from calling anyone in production except a designated production scheduling person to find out about delivery dates.
• Instruct sales reps not to promise deliveries that are unrealistic to avoid undermining credibility.
• Develop a better information system to detect sales trends early and report this information to production scheduling. The Sales VP should work with the sales reps to develop a system to gather this information.
• Revise the credit check system. A list of large, dependable customers should be provided to the production scheduling office and updated regularly so that reorders from these stores can be processed without making a new credit check each time.
• Conduct a study to estimate future sales and the implications of delivery time for lost sales and canceled orders.

What the Production VP Can Do

• Establish a better organized production scheduling office to handle all orders, reorders, and inquiries from sales reps.
• When information about sales trends is provided by the Sales VP, plan larger runs of popular items to build up inventories of these items.
• Establish a priority system to give favorable treatment to regular customers who place large orders. These customers would be identified before each season by the Sales VP.
• Explore the possibility that production scheduling would be facilitated and production costs kept at a minimum if all of the reorders were produced at one of the company's two plants.
• Look for opportunities to contract out some of the regular production of next-season lines in order to increase capacity for filling reorders. It is easier and cheaper to subcontract regular production than to try to find outside subcontractors to do rush jobs on reorders.
• Conduct a planning study on projected future production needs at KB, and compare costs and benefits for a variety of options including new plants, expanded plants, and more extensive subcontracting of production.

Save-Mart Role Play

How to Use the Exercise

The purpose of this role play is to allow students to practice the guidelines in Chapter 6 for delegating effectively. For this role play it is necessary to form three-person groups and determine for each group who will play the role of the boss, who will play the role of the subordinate, and who will serve as the observer. Any students who are left over may be used as extra observers.

After roles are assigned, give students copies of the materials relevant for their part in the role play exercise. All students should be given a copy of the general instructions and background information. Students selected to be managers should get a copy of their respective roles. Students selected to be observers should get a copy of the instructions for observers, the boss role, and the form for taking notes on the meeting. These notes will be the basis for feedback to the student playing the role of boss.

Before beginning the role play, allow time for students to read their materials and plan what to say. Remind students not to look at the role or materials for any other person, either before or during the role play. Information should be communicated only orally during the role play, and students should not show their printed role sheets to each other.

When the role playing is finished, reconvene the larger class to discuss what was learned. Ask observers for examples of especially effective behavior they witnessed. Identify the major difficulties faced by the managers in delegating to subordinates.

The total time for this exercise is about 50 minutes. It takes 5 minutes to explain the exercise and form triads. It takes about 10 minutes for students to read their materials and prepare for the role play. It takes about 15 minutes to do the actual role play, and another 5 minutes for feedback from the observer. The class discussion takes another 15 minutes.

General Instructions for Students

The purpose of this role play is to give you an opportunity to practice the guidelines in Chapter 6 for delegating effectively. This role play involves a meeting between the Vice President for Operations and one of the store managers who report to the VP. If you are selected to play the role of one of these managers, you will be provided with a description of your role. Before the role play begins, read the background information (see below) and study the description of your role. Try to imagine how the person would actually feel in that situation, and act accordingly during the role play. Please do not look at the instructions for any role other than the one that you are selected to play.

One or more observers will be assigned to each group. Students selected to be observers should read their instructions and the observer form for taking notes on the meeting. These notes will be the basis for giving feedback to the student who plays the role of the boss. Your instructor will provide additional information on procedures and time limits for the role play.

Background Information

Save-Mart is a retail discount chain with 20 stores in five states. The company was founded ten years ago and has been expanding rapidly. The stores are all identical in appearance and layout, and most of the stores are located in suburban areas. Merchandise is selected and purchased in large quantities by the headquarters buyers and stockpiled in the company's two warehouses. Each store receives an initial shipment of each item, then orders replacements as needed. All prices are set by headquarters marketing staff, and they also do the planning for all promotions and sales. Thus, all stores have the same prices and promotions going on simultaneously.

Save-Mart

Role For Vice President of Operations

You are the Vice President of Operations for Save-Mart. Top management has recently decided to experiment with decentralization of some important operating decisions. They feel that this change will improve sales and profits and reduce bureaucratic problems such as promotions that some stores do not need or are not prepared to handle. A few stores have been selected to participate in this trial because they have managers who appear to have the personality and ability required for an expanded managerial role. If after one year the changes appear successful, they will be instituted in all the Save-Mart stores. At that time, a program of bonuses based on store profits will be instituted for store managers.

You are about to meet with one of your subordinates, who is the manager of store number 17. The purpose of the meeting is to explain how more authority for decisions will be delegated to him or her. The following changes will be made:

1. The manager of store #17 will be given responsibility for pricing decisions and will be able to adjust prices upward or downward on all items in his/her store. Prices can be increased by up to 25% above the list price recommended by the headquarters Merchandise Department, and they can be reduced down to the base cost of an item.

2. Store #17 will still receive shipments of standard items, but the manager will be given authority to spend up to 20% of his/her merchandise replacement budget on items purchased from other suppliers rather than from the list of items available from Save-Mart warehouses. This flexibility will allow the store to sell items that have special appeal in its local area. Monthly sales reports on special items must be submitted to the Merchandise Vice President.

3. The manager of Store #17 will be able to conduct promotions campaigns and special sales in addition to the ones initiated by headquarters. A promotions budget will be provided to pay for the cost of local advertising in newspapers and on radio and television. The size of this budget will be determined next week. Headquarters should be informed in advance of local promotions and sales, to allow coordination with store-wide promotions.

Role for Manager of Store #17

You are about to meet with your boss, the Vice President of Store Operations. You have heard through the grapevine that some major changes are in the works to decentralize operating decisions to the level of the store managers. You are very excited about this change, because you believe that your store could increase sales and profits if you had more discretion about store operations. You have been hampered in competing with other stores in the same area by lack of control over prices and choice of items to sell. You do not have much expertise about advertising campaigns and would need some instruction and advice from the experts at headquarters to help you learn how to plan promotional campaigns. You are hoping that greater responsibility for profits will also mean greater opportunity to earn bonuses based on store profits. You enjoy working for Save-Mart, but you have an opportunity to take a job in another company with more responsibility and higher pay. You want to find out whether Save Mart is going to provide the opportunity to earn what you think you are worth.

Save-Mart

Instructions For Observers

Your job is to observe the role play and take notes on how well the student playing the role of boss followed the delegation guidelines presented in chapter 8. The relevant guidelines for this role play are listed on the observer form. Indicate whether the "boss" does each step and note examples of effective and ineffective behavior.

In preparation for the role play, read the background information and your copy of the role for the boss, so you can understand what information the boss should communicate to the subordinate.

Observer Form

1. Specifies responsibilities and authority clearly.   __Yes   __No
   Notes:

2. Checks for comprehension.   __Yes __No
   Notes:

3. Specifies reporting requirements.   __Yes __No
   Notes:

4. Ensures subordinate acceptance of responsibilities.   __Yes   __No
   Notes:

5. Offers support, assistance, and resources. __Yes __No
   Notes:

6. Other observations.

Union Chemicals Role Play

How to Use the Exercise

The objective of this role play exercise is to give students an opportunity to experience the difficulties in making a group decision when there are many uncertainties and strong pressure to reach a quick consensus. The role play involves a meeting of the CEO with five executives. Even though the group is not likely to be cohesive, the role play creates conditions like groupthink wherein potential pitfalls of the group's preferred solution are not assessed adequately.

After introducing the role play exercise, form six-person groups (composed of five managers and an observer) and identify a leader for each group by asking for volunteers or appointing somebody. Then assign the other four roles and select an observer. Any extra students left over after the groups are formed can serve as additional observers. Give each student a copy of the general instructions (including background information). Give students selected to be managers the descriptions of their roles. Remind students not to look at the materials for any other person, either before or during the role play. Give observers copies of the observer instructions, the observer key, and the observer form. Remind observers not to talk during the role play.

After the groups are formed, allow students time to study their roles and prepare for them. Remind students that they can interpret and embellish their roles as long as they do not introduce any factual information that changes the nature of the decision problem. Also, during the course of the discussion, they can change their position if it would be realistic to expect that they would do so in a real job situation. When students are ready, tell them that they have 30 minutes to make their decision, and start all of the groups at the same time.

After the groups have reached their decisions, reconvene the class to discuss the role play. Ask observers to report their group's decision and summarize it on the board. Then ask observers to describe the group process and evaluate how rational and systematic it was.

Total time for the exercise is a little more than an hour. It takes 5 minutes to form the groups, assign roles, and distribute materials; 10 minutes for students to study their written materials and prepare for the role play; 30 minutes for the role play, 10 minutes for feedback from observers, and 10 minutes for class discussion.

Union Chemicals

General Instructions for Students

The purpose of this role play is to provide an opportunity for you to experience what it is like to participate in a group that must make an important managerial decision. The role play also provides an opportunity to practice and strengthen skills that determine whether a decision group will be productive.

The role play involves a meeting of the five-member executive team. Students will be formed into groups, and each member of a group will be assigned a different role. If you are selected to be a manager, you will be given a description of your role. Before the role play begins, read the background information (below) and study the description of your role. Try to imagine how the person would actually feel in that situation and act accordingly during the role play. You may refer to your printed materials during the role play, if necessary, but do not show them to other people in the group. Please do not look at the materials for any role other than the one that you are assigned.

One or more observers will be assigned also to record the decision processes of each group. Observers should not talk to group members during the role play. An observer form will be provided to take notes that can be used to provide feedback to the group after the role play is completed. Your instructor will give you more information about procedures and time limits for this exercise.

Background Information

Union Chemicals is a large manufacturing company that makes chemicals, solvents, and various kinds of compounds. The company is financially sound, but sales have leveled off in the last few years and competition is increasing. The Product Research Department has developed a new bonding agent, and the executive group is meeting now to decide whether to begin marketing and production of the new product. The executive team includes the President, the VP-Research, the VP-Production, the VP-Marketing, and the VP-Finance.

Union Chemicals

Role for Company President

You have been President of Union Chemicals for three years. Under your leadership the company has been turned around from a condition of falling profits to one of modest but stable profits. You have aggressively encouraged expansion of research and development so that the company can remain competitive in an era of rapid technological change. Future growth for the company is dependent on sales of new or improved products, since demand for existing products is not increasing much and there is considerable foreign competition.

You have called the meeting for today to evaluate the prospects for a new bonding agent developed by Union's research scientists. The company holds patents on the basic process used to make the bonding agent. The specialized equipment needed to produce the new compound is available for purchase. The testing device necessary for quality control is made only by Eureka Corporation, one of your competitors, but you do not anticipate any problem in leasing their test device. You hope that the executive team will be able to reach a decision on the best course of action to follow.

Union Chemicals

Role For VP-Research

You have been Vice President of the Research and Development Department at Union Chemicals for ten years. Until the last few years the Research department was hampered by inadequate budgets. The company did not invest enough of its profits in development of new products, and this was a major reason for loss of sales to domestic and foreign competitors. However, there are several research projects underway currently, and the new bonding agent is farthest along toward final development. Product testing research has been going on for several months, and the results show that the new bonding agent is superior to any existing product on the market. In fact, the bonding agent is so strong and versatile that it can be used to bond materials that formerly had to be welded or fastened together mechanically. Nevertheless, just this week one of your junior scientists ran some tests that indicated the new compound may break down after a period of time when subjected to high temperatures, especially if the compound contains any impurities not detected and removed during production. More research is underway to determine the exact conditions under which problems may occur. You are hopeful about the prospects, because a successful new product would help your department get the larger research budgets you believe are necessary for the company to remain competitive in coming years.

Union Chemicals

Role for VP-Production

You have been VP of the Production Department for six years, during which time you have been very effective in minimizing production costs in order to keep the company competitive. The bonding agent developed by the Research Department is the first new product to come along in several years. In your opinion, going ahead with production would create some technical problems, but nothing insurmountable. Production of the bonding agent would require purchase of some new equipment which could not be used for existing products. The production equipment could be installed in six to eight weeks after it is delivered. A special quality control device to test for impurities could be leased from Eureka Corporation. Some new production employees would need to be hired, and anyone involved in making the new bonding agent would have to be trained to safely handle the extremely hazardous chemicals involved in the production process, in order to avoid accidents or an explosion. You enjoy the challenge of bringing a new product into regular production, and you are looking forward to getting started with pre-production planning as soon as possible.

Union Chemicals

Role for VP-Marketing

You have been VP for Marketing for two years, having been promoted to the position when your predecessor left for another job. You have been anxious to show what you can do to improve sales, but you have been frustrated by unfavorable market conditions and the lack of exciting new products. Now it looks like the company has finally come up with a winner. The new bonding agent could be sold to a variety of different industries, including home appliances, automobiles, building construction, aircraft construction, and military weapons systems. Your staff has projected a rapid sales growth for the new product, and it could become one of Union Chemical's most important products within a few years. You have just learned from reliable sources that Eureka Corporation, one of your competitors, is working on a similar product based on a different compound. You are concerned that any delay would mean losing the advantage of being first on the market with a new kind of product. You would like to begin planning a major marketing campaign for the new product as soon as possible.

Union Chemicals

Role for VP-Finance

You have been the VP for finance at Union Chemicals for five years and have worked for the company for nearly twenty years. Union badly needs a successful new product. Sales have leveled off in recent years, and competition keeps getting more intense. Just before this meeting, your staff gave you the financial projections for the current year, and profits are expected to decline by 10 percent. If the new bonding agent could be put on the market quickly, profits could be up again by the end of next year. You have already investigated the cost of purchasing new equipment to produce the bonding agent. The specialized production equipment would be very expensive, and the company would have to increase its long-term debt in order to finance the purchase. However, you are convinced that it would be an excellent investment. Production costs for the new product would be slightly higher than for other compounds currently made by the company, but because it is a unique product with no competitors, it could be sold at a premium price, yielding large profits. You strongly favor going ahead with marketing and production of the new product.

Union Chemicals

Instructions for Observers

Your assignment in this role play is to observe the group process and evaluate how effective it is. Before the role play begins, read the background information and the observer key. During the role play, pay particular attention to how well the group leader conducts the meeting. Use the Observer Form to take notes on effective and ineffective behavior by the group leader and other members. Use these notes to provide feedback to the leader and the group after the role play is completed.

Effective leaders encourage careful evaluation of the potential benefits and costs of selling the new product. Various members of the group have information about some serious risks associated with putting the new compound into immediate production. The potential risks should be identified and weighed carefully against the potential benefits to determine if the company should market the new product on a large scale, market it for limited (safe) applications only, or wait until further testing before going ahead with production and marketing. The leader should make sure dissenters have ample opportunity to be heard, and should encourage careful consideration of all potential problems. It is helpful for the leader to list pros and cons on a flipchart, blackboard, or summary sheet for group members to see.

A careful and systematic evaluation of pros and cons usually results in a cautious decision, such as continuing product testing to identify safe applications, or marketing the product only for limited use in low risk situations, perhaps with special clients who will experiment with it and help to evaluate its applications and limitations. Groups that do not use an effective decision process usually make a quick decision to proceed immediately with full scale production and unlimited marketing. Sometimes a cohesive group will exhibit the symptoms of groupthink; negative information is suppressed, ignored, or discounted, and anybody who expresses a dissenting opinion is pressured to go along with the majority position.

Observer Key for Union Chemicals Role Play

Summary of Potential Benefits

• Sales prospects are excellent due to many product applications and the uniqueness of the product.
• Profits would be large due to a high price and moderate costs.
• Production could be initiated in a relatively short period of time.
• The company needs a new product to boost sales and profits, which are beginning to lag.
• The new product would create enthusiasm and boost morale.

Summary of Potential Risks

• Cost of equipment is expensive and long term debt would be increased.
• The equipment could not be used for other purposes if production were delayed or interrupted.
• Some applications may not be feasible because the bonding agent will break down under high temperatures, subjecting the company to adverse publicity and expensive lawsuits.
• The new product requires handling of hazardous materials which could result in accidents or explosions, especially if production is rushed and employees are not properly trained.
• The competitor (Eureka Corporation) that is developing a similar product may split the market, making the compound less profitable than initially assumed.
• Because Eureka's is a likely competitor, they may refuse to allow Union Chemicals to license the test equipment necessary for quality control, thereby forcing delays in production until an alternative quality control process is developed. Even if Eureka is willing to lease the equipment, the cost may be so high that it will cut into profits from the new compound.

Observer Form for Union Chemicals Role Play

1. What did the company president do to facilitate the group's efforts to make a good decision?

2. What actions by the president (if any) hindered the group?

3. What effective or ineffective behaviors did other members exhibit?

4. What processes were used by the group to reach a decision? In what ways were they effective or ineffective?

Baxter Manufacturing Role Play

How to Use the Role Play

The purpose of this role play exercise is to give students an opportunity to experience what it is like to participate in a management group that is struggling to understand the reason for a complex and serious problem. It is a control-deviation problem where something has gone wrong and the group needs to diagnose the cause. Procedures for solving such problems are discussed briefly in Chapter 14. Unless effective procedures are followed, only about half of the groups will identify the cause before the time limit. Thus, one option is to provide a brief review of procedures for solving control-deviation problems before doing the role play.

The role play involves a meeting of the project manager and four other managers. After introducing the exercise, form six-person groups (composed of five managers and an observer) and identify a leader for each group by asking for volunteers or appointing somebody. Then assign the other four roles and select an observer; any extra students left over after the groups are formed can serve as additional observers.

Give students a copy of the background information and a copy of their role to study before beginning the role play. Remind students that all information should be communicated orally during the role play, and they should not look at the role for any other person, either before or during the role play.

Observers should be given a copy of the instructions for observers, (which includes a key to the problem analysis), and a copy of the observer form. Ask observers to use the form to take notes on effective and ineffective leadership behavior in the group. Observers should remain silent and not talk with group members during the role play. Afterward, the observers should provide feedback to the group about effective and ineffective leadership and group processes. Reconvene the class to get reports from the observers and discuss the exercise briefly.

The overall time required for the exercise is approximately I hour. It takes 5 minutes to explain the procedures and divide the class into groups, 10 minutes for students to read their materials and prepare for the role play, 30 minutes for the role play itself, and 15 minutes for feedback from observers and general class discussion.

Baxter Manufacturing

Instructions for Students

The purpose of this role play exercise is to give you an opportunity to experience what it is like to participate in a management group that is struggling to understand the reason for a complex and serious problem. The role play involves a problem solving meeting held by a project manager with four other managers in the project team.

For this exercise, students will be formed into groups, and each student member will be assigned a different role to play. If you are selected to be a manager, you will be given a description of your role. Before beginning the role play, read the background information and the instructions for your role. Do not look at the instructions for any other role than the one you have been assigned. During the role play, you may communicate orally any information in your written materials to other members of the group, but do not let them read your written materials. Note that the information available to the group is sufficient to diagnose the likely cause of the problem.

One or two observers will be assigned to each group to record the group's problem solving processes. The observers should not talk to group members during the role play. Observers will be given a form to take notes that can be used to provide feedback to the group after the role play is completed. Your instructor will provide more information about procedures for doing this exercise and time limits.

Baxter Manufacturing

Background Information

Baxter is a small manufacturing company that makes specialized electronic components for aerospace companies. The company has a major contract to manufacture a guidance system unit for missiles. Baxter assembles the guidance system units, using some components that are made in house as well as some components that are purchased from other companies. The completed units are shipped to the client where they are subjected to extensive tests under simulated conditions. Any units that fail these tests are returned to Baxter to be reworked. The rework process involves elaborate checking and it costs almost as much as the initial production. Moreover, only one or two reworks a month can be done without disrupting regular production.

Production on this project started in July. It is now the first week in December and Baxter is behind schedule in delivery of acceptable units. The table below shows the number of units needed, produced and delivered, accepted, reworked, and delinquent for each month of production.

	July	Aug.	Sept.	Oct.	Nov.	Dec.	Jan.	Feb.	Mar.
Amount needed	20	20	20	20	30	30	30	30	30
Amount produced	20	20	20	20	30				
Amount accepted	19	19	20	20	25				
Amount reworked	0	0	1	1	0				
Amount delinquent	1	2	1	0	5				

The Project Manager for the guidance system project has called a meeting of the key managers involved in the project to identify the cause of the problem and find a solution. Attending the meeting are the following people:

1. Project Manager
2. Production Manager
3. Engineering Manager
4. Purchasing Manager
5. Human Resource Manager

Baxter Manufacturing

Role For Project Manager

It is your responsibility to supervise the guidance system project, coordinate the contributions of different departments, and keep the project on schedule. The guidance system units are produced on two assembly lines. Assembly Lines 1 and 2 are used during the day shift, but only Assembly Line 2 is used at night. There are twice as many employees on the day shift as on the night shift. The day shift has been working at full capacity since the project began and it produces twice as many units as the night shift.

The project has had a troubled history. The production schedule now in effect provides for only the minimum number of units needed each month. If any units are rejected by the client, the project will fall behind schedule. As the summary table shows, some rejections occurred in July and August. That problem was traced to the equipment used in adjusting the tracking sensors on Assembly Line 1. This adjustment is a critical step in the production process, since proper adjustment is essential for the guidance system to perform adequately. The problem was solved in September by purchasing better equipment that allowed the tracking sensors to be adjusted to the specific tolerances. By the end of October, the project was back on schedule. Then, in November, rejects started occurring again, this time more drastically. The reason for the recent rejects is not known, and people have different opinions about the likely cause.

You have called a meeting of managers who have the information needed to identify the cause of the problem. Your task is to run the meeting in an efficient manner. The group has 30 minutes to discover why the reject rate has increased and find a solution.

Baxter Manufacturing

Role for Production Manager

It is your responsibility to supervise the manufacture of components and the assembly of the guidance units, using components made in house and components purchased outside. Production was initially done on the day shift by 20 employees using Assembly Lines 1 and 2. Then in January, when production was scheduled to increase by 50%, a night shift was added with 10 workers using Assembly Line 2. Some day-shift workers were moved to the night shift, because it was necessary to have some experienced workers on both shifts to operate critical equipment and to help train the new workers.

Starting the night shift has not been as smooth as you had hoped. A rash of problems have occurred at night, including worker complaints, fights, and accidents. For example, the first week a careless worker ran his forklift into the electrical transformer and cut off the supply of power to the entire plant. Production was disrupted for two hours until repairs could be made. The transformer is still not working properly, and some of the heavy machinery in the plant that is operated only at night causes power surges when it is turned on and off.

The night shift is supervised by your assistant production manager, who formerly ran Assembly line 2 on the day shift. You wonder if he has enough experience to deal with the special problems on the night shift. You are considering moving to the night shift yourself for a while to get things under control.

Baxter Manufacturing

Role for Engineering Manager

One of your responsibilities is to supervise the adjustment of the tracking sensors after the components for the guidance system are assembled. The adjustment is done with some specialized equipment that is extremely sensitive. Each assembly line has its own machines for adjusting tracking sensors. New equipment was purchased in August for Assembly Line 1, because the old equipment did not allow adjustments to be made to the necessary tolerance levels. The deficiency in this equipment was the cause of the rejected units in July and August, both of which were produced on Assembly Line 1. There were no more rejects on Assembly Line 1 after the new equipment was installed.

You have investigated the source of the rejects in November. They all occurred for units produced on Assembly Line 2 on the night shift. As in the case of the earlier rejects, you suspect that the cause may have something to do with the equipment used to adjust the tracking sensors. Although the present equipment on Assembly Line 2 allows operators to set tolerances to specified levels, it is several years old and may not be as reliable as it used to be. You favor replacing it with new equipment like that purchased for Assembly Line 1. In the meantime, Assembly Line 1 will be used for aspects of the rework that must be done on a regular assembly line to be safe.

Baxter Manufacturing

Role for Purchasing Manager

Your responsibility is to purchase the materials, components, and equipment used in production of guidance system units and other products made by Baxter. You are very pleased with the success of the equipment you purchased for Assembly Line 1 to replace the old equipment that caused the rejects in July and August. Although the new equipment was very expensive ($40,000), it has several advantages: it allows closer tolerances to be set, it is faster, it provides better protection against power surges, and it is easier to maintain. However, in comparison to the older equipment, the new equipment requires more skill, so it is important to use experienced and responsible workers to operate it.

You suspect that the new rash of rejects may be due to the use of inferior materials in producing the tracking sensors. The current supplier of materials for the guidance system project was selected because the supplier has a good reputation and the lowest price. However, you have subsequently heard that the supplier is having financial problems, and you wonder if the quality of their materials has suffered as a result. To test the materials would take a couple of weeks. You know of an alternative supplier, but the materials would cost about 40% more if purchased from that company.

Baxter Manufacturing

Role for Human Resource Manager

It is your responsibility to hire and train workers for Baxter Manufacturing, to manage the pay and benefits system, and to handle day-to-day union matters and grievances. You have been very busy during September and October helping to prepare for the initiation of the night shift. The night shift was staffed by 6 of the day shift workers and 4 new workers. An additional 6 new workers were hired for the day shift to replace those who were moved to the night. You hired the ten new workers and supervised their initial training. Additional on-the-job training of new workers is being provided by the experienced workers on both shifts.

The employees that moved from the day shift to the night shift were very unhappy about the change, because they do not like working nights. It is difficult to adjust to a different work schedule, and there are a number of things that make the work more tedious and unpleasant at night. The workers miss seeing their friends who are still on the day shift. It is much noisier due to some heavy machinery in another part of the plant that is only operated at night. The company cafeteria is not open at night, and only vending machine food is available. A couple of the workers who were switched have been complaining to the union that they should get extra pay for having to work at night.

You have just learned that the defective units were all produced by the night shift. You suspect that the quality problems in the guidance units may be related to dissatisfaction among the workers who were moved from the day to the night shift. Workers who are upset are likely to be less careful about quality.

Instructions for Observers

The type of problem the group must solve is a control-deviation problem; something has gone wrong and the group needs to diagnose the cause. The cause of the problem is explained on the answer key (see below). Before the role play begins, read the background material and the answer key.

Your assignment during this role play is to observe the group process and make notes describing it on the Observer Form. Do not say anything to the group during the role play (don't give them any clues), and do not let members of the group see the answer key until they are finished with the role play. Afterward, give feedback to the group about their group process and things the leader did that helped or hindered the group in identifying the problem and dealing with it.

Key For Problem Analysis

The difficult part of this type of problem solving is the problem diagnosis, not the solution generation and evaluation. The necessary information to diagnose the problem is distributed among the members of the group, but no single member has all of the necessary information. The leader should keep the discussion focused on analyzing this information. Pay particular attention to the way the leader conducts and structures the discussion to solve the problem. Effective leaders seek to identify in detail the deviations between actual and desired (normal) conditions with respect to their location, duration, frequency, and magnitude. Then they look for a single cause that will account for the deviations. If none is evident, they look for two or more causes that together produce the deviations. Once the cause of the problem is correctly diagnosed, it will be evident how to deal with it. The leader should make sure responsibility is assigned for dealing with the problem.

Cause of the problem

The power surges on the night shift interfere with the equipment used to adjust the tracking sensors on Assembly Line 2. The power surges are due to the damaged transformer in combination with switching heavy machinery on and off, which occurs only at night. Power surges in the daytime are not strong enough to disrupt the equipment.

Solutions to the Problem

An immediate and inexpensive solution is to use Assembly Line 1 at night, since the new equipment is better protected against power surges. This solution may require some shifting of personnel familiar with the new equipment from the day shift to the night shift. An alternative solution is to replace the transformer, but this may take a few weeks and would be moderately expensive. However, replacing the transformer may be desirable for other reasons also. Management should assess whether the faulty transformer is causing any other problems. Finally, it may be worthwhile to try again to repair the transformer before deciding to purchase a replacement.

Reasons why other factors are not the cause

1. Defective materials: The same materials are used on both day and night shifts.

2. Old, worn equipment: The equipment on Assembly Line 2 works okay on the day shift, it is defective only at night.

3. Mistakes are made by inexperienced workers on the night shift. There are as many new workers on the day shift, which has no rejects. Also, the new workers do not perform critical functions likely to cause rejects.

4. The night shift manager lacks experience. This is not likely to be a problem. The manager has prior experience in running Assembly line 2 during the day shift. The only unique conditions at night are the larger number of new employees and the dissatisfaction of some employees who were moved from the day shift.

5. The quality problems are caused by dissatisfied workers on the night shift. There is insufficient evidence of a causal relationship between dissatisfaction and quality problems, and this type of dissatisfaction seldom results in such an abrupt and sharp decline in quality. However, to avoid potential problems due to dissatisfaction about working on the night shift, the company should ask for volunteers rather than arbitrarily assigning workers to this shift, and management should consider offering a small pay differential as an incentive to night workers.

Observer Form for Baxter Manufacturing Role Play

1. What did the project manager do to facilitate the group's efforts to analyze and solve the problem?

2. What actions by the project manager (if any) hindered the group?

3. What effective or ineffective behaviors did other members exhibit?

4. What processes were used by the group to analyze and solve the problem? In what way were they effective or ineffective?

Other Exercises

Description of the Supplementary Exercises

This section of the Instructor's Manual contains four supplementary exercises that can be used with the leadership book. As with the role plays, these exercises are merely examples of the types of experiential exercises that can be used to facilitate learning and make a course on managerial leadership more interesting. There was not sufficient space in the manual to include exercises on every subject. The in-basket exercise is primarily relevant for Chapter 2, and it was included to help students appreciate the challenges faced by leaders in managing their time wisely. The exercise on Identifying Managerial Practices was included to help students learn the definitions of the fourteen managerial practices introduced in Chapter 3 and discussed in Chapters 4 and 5. The Planning Exercise was included to help students appreciate the difficulties of planning complex projects and activities, as discussed in Chapter 4. The Supportive Listening Exercise was provided to give students an opportunity to test their understanding of supportive communication principles in Chapter 5. Other supplementary exercises like these can be found in many available books on experiential learning in management and organization behavior (e.g., Whetten and Cameron, *Developing Managerial Skills*, HarperCollins, 1991).

In-Basket Exercise

How to Use the Exercise

The purpose of this modified in-basket exercise is to provide students with practice in thinking about priorities and planning daily activities. The exercise is especially relevant for students who have never held a job as a manager or supervisor. The exercise should be done alone by students, in class or as homework (it takes about half an hour). To use this exercise, it is necessary to duplicate copies of the following parts for students (a total of 5 pages per student): Instructions for the In-Basket Exercise, the In-Basket Items, and the Plans for Tomorrow.

After students complete the exercise, it should be discussed in class, using one of the following options.

Option 1: Form groups of 3-5 students to discuss the exercise and compare answers. After the groups are finished, ask the groups to report any major unresolved disagreements and discuss them. This option takes about 30 minutes for group work and another 15 minutes for class discussion.

Option 2: Discuss the exercise in the larger class rather than breaking into small groups. For each item, ask for a volunteer to say how it was handled and the priority rating given to it. Ask if anybody handled the item in a different way. Remember that for most items there is not a single correct way. Ask students to examine whether they delegated enough items and concentrated on items relevant to their presumed key objectives. This option takes about 30 minutes.

A possible followup exercise is to ask students to apply some of the time management principles to their own daily and weekly planning. For example, students could develop a list of objectives and priorities, keep activity logs to see how they spend their time, make daily activity lists, and keep notes in a journal on any incidents of procrastination and wasted time.

Instructions for In-Basket Exercise

The purpose of this exercise is to provide practice in thinking about priorities and planning activities for the next day. Assume you are a regional sales manager in a large corporation. You have been away on a business trip since Monday, and you have returned a day early. It is now 4:30 P.M. on Thursday and you are in your office to look at your mail and plan some activities for the next day. Since you had expected to be away until Friday night, no meetings or appointments are scheduled for you at your office tomorrow. You have only half an hour to make your plans, because you have to meet your spouse for dinner.

The company has three major product lines, and each product line has several different models. Your regional sales office is housed in a company facility that includes other regional departments (e.g., personnel, accounting, distribution, maintenance), a large production facility, and a warehouse for company products. Your boss, the Sales Vice President, is located at corporate headquarters in another state. You have twenty sales representatives who report to you and an office staff of five employees who process orders sent in by the sales representatives. In addition, you have an assistant sales manager and a secretary.

In your in-basket are the following items. Read through the items, then use the form to indicate the things you would plan to do tomorrow (Friday). Remember, this is a timed exercise and you have only 30 minutes to make your plans. If the exercise is done in class, your instructor will tell you when to begin.

In-Basket Items

1. Memo from Barbara Sawyer, one of your sales representatives, asking for permission to attend a one-day course on the company's new fax machine. The course is next week, and she needs to have a decision by Monday. She notes that two other sales representatives from your office will be attending the course.

2. Letter from a major customer complaining about quality defects in the Model 1140 copier purchased earlier this year.

3. Note from your secretary reminding you that the monthly sales report is due at corporate headquarters this coming Wednesday.

4. Memo from Sharon Maroni, one of the sales representatives, asking for her company car to be replaced by a new one. Ever since it was rammed by a truck last month, the car keeps breaking down, leaving her stranded in remote areas.

5. Memo from the vice president for human resources, asking you to recommend somebody as a candidate for the new regional office in Alabama and provide background information on the person's qualifications. He wants each regional manager to identify the most promising candidate in his or her region. This information is needed in two weeks.

6. Note from your assistant manager requesting a meeting with you to discuss a new marketing proposal.

7. Note from your secretary informing you that your boss called and scheduled a meeting on Tuesday of next week to decide the sales goals for your region.

8. Memo to all regional managers from the Sales Vice President requesting them to gather information about reasons for the recent decline in sales of Model 1140 copiers. The subject will be discussed at the meeting of regional managers in two weeks.

9. Telephone message from a sales representative--Tom Jones--saying that a major corporation will order a large quantity of printers if some modifications can be made in them. Tom wants to know if the modifications are feasible. He asked you to call him back for details.

10. Letter from bank requesting verification of employment for one of your office staff. Employment verifications are handled by the Personnel Office.

11. Memo from Lloyd Denton, one of your office staff, complaining that there are no longer enough spaces in the employee parking lot since the expansion of the production facility. The production employees start work early, and all the spaces are gone by the time the sales staff arrive. Parking is the responsibility of the Facilities Manager.

12. Telephone message from George Palmer, one of your sales representatives, asking you to check into reasons for delay in delivery of printers to a customer who is threatening to cancel the order. Delivery is the responsibility of the Distribution Manager.

13. Letter from local resident complaining about the noise from the plant.

14. Memo from the training director at corporate headquarters, suggesting development of a training program for office staff in the new computer program being developed for processing orders.

15. Letter from a customer expressing appreciation that one of the sales representatives, Joe Owens, was so helpful in solving a technical problem for them.

16. Memo from the headquarters marketing department with a sample brochure attached for your review. No deadline given. It usually takes about half an hour to review a brochure and write comments.

17. Letter from an important customer inquiring about prices on the new fax machines to be introduced next month.

18. Telephone message from a sales representative--Gwen Gordon--asking you to look into a mistake involving her health care benefits.

19. Expense authorization from a sales representative for your approval and signature. These forms are forwarded to accounting with your signature, and a copy remains in your sales office.

20. Telephone note about a call from a business reporter at a local paper wanting to interview you about the company's new fax machine.

Plans for Tomorrow

Indicate what things you would do in each category (use item number to reference in-basket). Indicate the priority in parentheses after the item, using the following ratings:

A   High priority, both important and urgent, do tomorrow if possible.

B   Moderate priority, important but not urgent, or urgent but only moderately important, do tomorrow only if time available.

C   Low priority, neither important nor urgent, or something that is the responsibility of someone in another unit.

Things to Do Yourself

Responsibilities to Delegate (to whom?)

Meetings or Appointments for Tomorrow (with whom?)

Telephone Calls (to whom about what?)

Memos, Letters, or Notes to Write (to whom about what?)

Items to File, Hold, or Forward

The priority for each item is based on consideration of importance and urgency. Priority ratings range from A to C. Priority A items are important and urgent; they should be done first on Friday. Priority B items are important but less urgent; they should be done Friday if there is enough time, otherwise, they can be done the following week. The priority C items are least urgent, and they include less important things that can be put off, or things that can be passed on to others because they are not part of the manager's job responsibilities. Note that assignment of priorities is somewhat arbitrary, because it depends on a manager's objectives, which vary from person to person. The priorities indicated here are only intended to provide some general guidance.

Things to Do Yourself

• Review information needed to set quarterly sales goals at the Tuesday meeting with your boss. Do it tomorrow to allow time to gather additional information if necessary before Tuesday. (item #7; priority A)
• Review potential candidates for promotion to the new regional office. This is important but not urgent, because the meeting is not for two weeks. (item #5; priority B)
• Investigate feasibility of getting a new or better company car for Sharon Maroni. This is important, but it may be put off until next week if necessary. (item #4; priority B)
• Investigate how serious the parking problem is by talking to your office staff about it when the opportunity arises. (item #11; priority C)
• Find out when the sample brochure is needed by the headquarters marketing department the next time you talk to them; most likely there is no rush, because no deadline was indicated. (item #16; priority C)

Responsibilities to Delegate (to whom?)

• Ask your secretary (or assistant manager) to assemble information tomorrow so that on Monday you can write the monthly sales report due Wednesday. (item #3; priority A)
• Ask your assistant manager to gather information about the declining sales of Model 1140 copiers. This is important but not urgent, because the meeting is not for two weeks. (item #8; priority B)
• Ask the sales representative in the local area to meet with the customer who made complaints about the Model 1140 copier and report

the nature of the problem; quality problems may be related to declining sales. (item #2; priority B)

• Ask your secretary to prepare a short letter to send with a brochure listing prices on the new fax machines to the customer who inquired about them, then have her give the sales representative in that district a copy of the letter with a note asking him to follow up with the potential customer. (item #17; priority B)

• Ask your secretary (or assistant manager) to check into the problem in health care benefits for Gwen Gordon. (item #18; priority B)

Meetings to Hold Tomorrow (with whom?)

• Meet with your secretary first thing in the morning to delegate tasks and to dictate some letters and memos. (priority A)

• Meet with your assistant to delegate tasks (priority A). Use this meeting also to get opinions about what the regional sales goals should be, and to discuss her marketing proposal (item #6; priority B).

Telephone Calls to Make Tomorrow (to whom about what?)

• Call distribution manager to check into reason for delay in delivery of printers; then call George Palmer with an answer. (item #12; priority A)

• Call Tom Jones to get more information about modifications wanted in printers by a potential major customer. Then call production manager to discuss feasibility of modifications; if necessary arrange a meeting. (item #9; priority A)

• Call Barbara Sawyer to convey your decision on her request to attend the training course; note short deadline. (item #1; priority A)

• Call back the reporter (or arrange an appointment) to discuss the new fax machine. (item #20; priority B).

Memos or Letters To Write (to whom about what?)

• Dictate a memo to sales representatives asking them for information about customer complaints and reactions to Model 1140 copiers by the end of next week, with copy to your assistant. (item #8; priority A)

• Respond to training director with memo on the training program for office staff. (item #14; priority B)

• Pass on to Joe Owen, one of your sales reps, the letter from a customer praising him, with a note of your own complimenting him. (item #15; priority B)

121

Other Items To File, Hold, or Forward

• Hold sample brochure until you find out when it is needed and have a free half hour to review it and make comments. (make notation on reminder list). (item #16; priority B)
• Sign expense authorization and give to secretary to forward to accounting. (item #19; priority B)
• Pass on request for verification of employment to personnel office. (item #10; priority C)
• Pass on complaint about noise to plant manager's office. (item #13; priority C)

Exercise on Identifying Managerial Practices

How to Use the Exercise

This short quiz gives students an opportunity to assess their understanding of the fourteen managerial practices described in Chapter 3. To use this exercise it is necessary to make and distribute copies (a total of 4 pages per student) of the instructions for students and the lists of effective and ineffective behaviors. Students should do the exercise alone, either in class or as homework (it takes about 10 to 15 minutes). Afterward, announce the correct answers and discuss any items missed by a significant number of people. The scoring and discussion usually take about 15 minutes. When discussing the answers it is useful to remind students that most descriptions of managerial behavior are multi-dimensional and involve more than a single behavior category. Some students may fail to identify the most salient managerial practice in an item but may recognize another managerial practice that is also represented in the item.

Scoring Key

Effective Behavior	Ineffective Behavior
1. INFO	15. CONS
2. MON	16. PS
3. CONS	17. CLR
4. MC	18. DEV
5. PLN	19. RWD
6. MOT	20. MC
7. CLR	21. MOT
8. SUP	22. REC
9. PS	23. NET
10. REC	24. SUP
11. NET	25. PLN
12. RWD	26. DEL
13. SUP	27. MON
14. DEV	28. INFO

Identifying Managerial Practices

Instructions for Students

The purpose of this exercise is to develop a better understanding of the fourteen managerial practices in the Yukl taxonomy, described in Chapter 3. The exercise consists of behavior descriptions mixed up in random order. The first set of items includes examples of effective behavior, and the second set includes examples of ineffective behavior. Your task is to identify the managerial practice best depicted by each behavior example and write the code for that practice on the line next to the item. The codes and definitions of each practice are as follows:

PLN   PLANNING: determining long term objectives and strategies, allocating resources according to priorities, determining how to use personnel and resources to accomplish a task efficiently, and determining how to improve coordination, productivity, and the effectiveness of the organizational unit.

PS   PROBLEM SOLVING: identifying work-related problems, analyzing problems in a timely but systematic manner to identify causes and find solutions, and acting decisively to resolve important problems or crises.

CLR   CLARIFYING ROLES AND OBJECTIVES: assigning tasks, providing direction in how to do the work, and communicating a clear understanding of job responsibilities, task objectives, deadlines, and performance expectations.

INFO   INFORMING: disseminating relevant information about decisions, plans, and activities to people that need it to do their work, providing written materials and documents, and answering requests for technical information.

MON   MONITORING: gathering information about work activities and external conditions affecting the work, checking on the progress and quality of the work, evaluating the performance of individuals and the organizational unit, analyzing trends and forecasting external events.

MOT   MOTIVATING: using influence techniques that appeal to emotion or logic to generate enthusiasm for the work, commitment to task objectives, and compliance with requests for cooperation, assistance, support, or resources; setting an example of appropriate behavior.

CONS   CONSULTING: checking with people before making changes that affect them, encouraging suggestions for improvement, inviting participation in decision making, incorporating the ideas and suggestions of others in decisions.

DEL   DELEGATING: allowing subordinates to have substantial responsibility and discretion in carrying out work activities, handling problems, and making important decisions.

SUP   SUPPORTING: acting friendly and considerate, being patient and helpful, showing sympathy and support when someone is upset or anxious, listening to complaints and problems, looking out for someone's interests.

DEV   DEVELOPING: providing coaching and helpful career advice, and doing things to facilitate a person's skill acquisition, professional development, and career advancement.

MC   MANAGING CONFLICT AND TEAM BUILDING: facilitating the constructive resolution of conflict, and encouraging cooperation, teamwork, and identification with the work unit.

NET   NETWORKING: socializing informally, developing contacts with people who are a source of information and support, and maintaining contacts through periodic interaction, including visits, telephone calls, correspondence, and attendance at meetings and social events.

REC   RECOGNIZING: providing praise and recognition for effective performance, significant achievements, and special contributions; expressing appreciation for someone's contributions and special efforts.

REW   REWARDING: providing or recommending tangible rewards such as a pay increase or promotion for effective performance, significant achievements, and demonstrated competence.

Examples of Effective Behavior

____ 1. Explains the changes in the company's new health benefits plan.

____ 2. Walks around to observe how the work is going.

____ 3. Asks for ideas about improving the new marketing plan.

____ 4. Reminds members of the team that they depend on each other and must cooperate to complete the project successfully.

____ 5. Determines in advance what resources are needed to carry out a new project.

____ 6. Holds a meeting to talk about how vital the new contract is for the company and tells us that we can meet the difficult terms if we all do our part.

____ 7. Establishes performance goals for each important aspect of the department's work.

____ 8. Tells me to handle my new account any way I think is best.

____ 9. Acts decisively in dealing with equipment breakdowns so that little time is lost in production.

____10. Tells me why she considers my performance last quarter to be exceptional.

____11. Calls a manager in another work unit to offer assistance in dealing with a problem.

____12. Recommends a promotion for the product manager with the best performance record last year.

____13. Takes the time to listen to a subordinate with a personal problem or complaint.

____14. Lets me conduct some of the project meetings so that I can acquire more managerial experience.

Examples of Ineffective Behavior

____15. Asks for suggestions, then makes an arbitrary decision that ignores them.

____16. Jumps to conclusions about the cause of a problem on the basis of insufficient information.

____17. Gives contradictory directions when assigning a task.

____18. Gives all the challenging assignments to his most experienced subordinate rather than allowing other subordinates an opportunity to learn how to handle them.

____19. Gives pay increases to her friends even when they have low performance.

____20. Says things to foster distrust and hostility between two members of the department.

____21. Sets a poor example by leaving early when there is important work to finish.

____22. Looks for something to criticize rather than complimenting a person for successfully completing a difficult assignment.

____23. Finds excuses for not attending social and ceremonial events held by the organization.

____24. Blows up and insults a subordinate in front of other people.

____25. Forgets to order some of the materials needed by the department for a new project.

____26. Demands that subordinate managers get his approval before taking action to deal with any problems in their departments.

____27. Fails to follow up to verify that a request was carried out.

____28. Forgets to tell me in advance about an important meeting that I should attend.

Planning Exercise

How to Use the Exercise

This exercise allows students an opportunity to carry out a fairly simple planning task that will help them understand planning concepts and procedures. To use this exercise it is necessary to make and distribute copies (a total of 3 pages) of the instructions for students and the forms for developing an activity list and an event calendar. Students should do the exercise alone as homework or in small groups during class. It takes about 20 to 30 minutes to read the instructions and fill out the activity list and event calendar. The followup discussion should focus on major problems and issues in this type of planning. About 15 to 20 minutes are needed for the class discussion.

There are no exact answers for this exercise, but some plans are better than others. Evaluation of plans should consider the following things:

• Are activities sequenced in logical order within and across the major subtasks?

• Are arrangements that require availability of people or facilities made far enough in advance to insure some choice?

• Does the student check on alternatives before selecting subcontractors for major activities (e.g., band, print shop, caterer)?

• Does the student attend to details that are important but not obvious?

• Does the student check on preparations where appropriate?

Planning Exercise

Instructions for Students

The purpose of this exercise is to provide an opportunity to carry out a relatively simple planning task that demonstrates some of the types of judgments and analyses necessary to plan more complex projects and activities. Assume that it is now March and you have been asked by your boss to arrange a dinner dance for the approximately one hundred employees of his department and their spouses. He has selected a site for the event, but there is still some flexibility on the date. If possible, your boss would like to have the event some evening during the first two weeks in June, but this is a time when this site is popular for weddings and receptions.

A separate caterer must be arranged, since the site does not provide food service, only bar service for drinks. Your boss would like to have formal, printed announcements (with RSVP's) sent out at least three weeks before the event to get an accurate count of how many people will attend it. Your boss wants to have a live band for entertainment. Assume that you have a limited budget and must check on prices for everything except the site.

In planning the dinner there are four major subtasks (e.g., site arrangements, dinner arrangements, entertainment arrangements, and invitations). Identify the component action steps for each subtask and list them in the proper sequence on the Activity Lists. Next to each action step write your estimate of how long it would take to do that action step (hours or days). Determine how much lead time is necessary for starting each action step. Assume two weeks turnaround for a print shop to print invitations. Identify any dependencies between action steps in different subtasks. A flow chart of action steps is helpful, but it is possible to do the event calendar without a flow chart. Then complete the event calendar by indicating the week in which each action step should occur. The event calendar should show all of the action steps for the four subtasks arranged in a logical sequence. Assume that the dinner dance will occur in the twelfth week after planning begins.

Activity List for Dinner Dance Plans

Site Arrangements

Dinner Arrangements

Guest List and Invitations

Entertainment

Event Calendar for Dinner Dance Plans

Week 1

Week 2

Week 3

Week 4

Week 5

Week 6

Week 7

Week 8

Week 9

Week 10

Week 11

Week 12   Dinner dance is held

Key for Planning Exercise

Sample Activity Lists

Site Arrangements

1. Select potential dates
2. Check availability of site
3. Select date and reserve site
4. Plan site preparation (tables, decorations, open bar, bartenders)
5. Check site preparation (just before event)

Food and Drink Arrangements

1. Check menu choices and prices with potential caterers
2. Select caterer and reserve date
3. Select dinner menu, snacks, drinks
4. Tell caterer the final estimate on number of guests
5. Plan seating arrangements (optional)
6. Check with caterer on final preparations

Guest List and Invitations

1. Prepare guest list
2. Determine information to put on invitations
3. Check prices at print shops
4. Select print shop
5. Pick up invitations from print shop
6. Prepare and mail invitations
7. Keep record of RSVP's
8. Determine final guest list

Entertainment

1. Determine type of music and potential bands
2. Find out availability and prices of bands
3. Select and hire a band
4. Plan door prizes and purchase them (optional)
5. Check on band
6. Bring door prizes to site

Sample Event Calendar

Week 1   Select potential dates
             Check availability of site
             Select date and reserve site

Week 2   Prepare guest list
             Check menu choices and prices with potential caterers
             Determine type of music and potential bands
             Find out availability and prices of bands

Week 3   Select caterer and reserve date
             Select dinner menu, snacks, drinks
             Determine information to put on invitations
             Check print shop prices
             Select and hire a band

Week 4   Select print shop
             Plan door prizes and purchase them (optional)

Week 5   Plan site preparation (tables, decorations, bars, bartenders)

Week 6   Pick up invitations from print shop
             Prepare and mail invitations

Week 7   Record RSVP's

Week 8   Record RSVP's

Week 9   Record RSVP's

Week 10   Determine final guest list
             Tell caterer final estimate on number of guests
             Plan seating arrangements

Week 11   Check with caterer on final preparations
             Check on site preparation
             Check on band
             Bring door prizes to site

Week 12   Dinner dance is held

Exercise on Supportive Communication

How to Use the Exercise

This short exercise is designed to help students understand the concepts and guidelines on supportive communication. To use the exercise it is necessary to make copies of it for students (it is only 2 pages). Ask students to do the exercise alone, either in class or as homework. Each part takes about 5 -10 minutes.

After students have completed the exercises, they should be discussed in class. Ask students to evaluate each response in Part 1 and say how they would respond in this situation. Consider the best sequence or combination of responses. Use the same procedure for Part 2. The class discussion should take about 15 minutes.

Exercise on Supportive Communication

The purpose of this exercise is to provide a better understanding of supportive communication (see Chapter 5).

Part 1

Assume that you are an office manager in a large insurance company. You have 12 subordinates who process claims. One of your subordinates, Joe McDonald, has been in his current job for only a few weeks and he is having problems learning how to operate the computer. You are meeting with him to discuss this problem. Joe says, "I just can't seem to learn how to use the software program correctly. I tried to get somebody to explain it to me, but the other people in the office are not very helpful. They don't pay any attention to me and seem very annoyed when I ask questions."

Some possible responses to Joe are listed below. In the space beneath each response, explain briefly why it is appropriate or inappropriate in terms of the guidelines on supportive communication.

1. "The computer is complicated, and it takes a while to learn how to use the new software. Hang in there and keep trying."

2. "You are not trying hard enough. You should spend more time studying the manuals and practicing entries."

3. "I will show you how to use the software. You work on the computer for a while and I will watch to see what you are doing wrong."

4. "I will tell one of the other workers to help you."

5. "Why do you think the other employees won't help you?"

6. "You feel that the other employees in the office don't pay any attention to you?"

Part 2

Another subordinate--Jane Jarvis--seems very upset, and you ask her what is wrong. She replied that her car broke down on the highway, and she had to walk a mile in the rain to a gas station to get help. As she was walking along the highway, she twisted her ankle and ruined her expensive new shoes in the mud. She got to work late and is behind on an important claims report due today. Her ankle is sore and she is having a hard time concentrating on the report.

Some possible responses to Jane are listed below. In the space beneath each response, explain briefly why it is appropriate or inappropriate in terms of the guidelines on supportive communication and the need to show concern for both the task and people.

1. "It's been a rough day for you, Jane, but that claims report still has to be completed today."

2. "You think that's bad. Let me tell you what happened to me yesterday."

3. "Jane, we need to talk about the schedule for testing the new software."

4. "You can't let these things get you down. Try to forget about it and concentrate on your work."

5. "You must be really upset."

6. "Is there something I can do to help you with the report?"

Exercise on Supportive Communication

Answer Key for Part 1

1. "The computer is complicated, and it takes a while to learn how to use the new software. Hang in there and keep trying."

This response shows sympathy, but it does nothing to discover the nature of Allan's problems with the computer or with coworkers.

2. "You are not trying hard enough. You should spend more time studying the manuals and practicing entries."

This response is very evaluative. The manager is blaming Allan for the problem with the computer, and is ignoring the problem with coworkers.

3. "I will show you how to use the software. You work on the computer for a while and I will watch to see what you are doing wrong."

This response seeks to learn why Allan is having trouble with the computer, but it ignores the problem with coworkers.

4. "I will tell one of the other workers to help you."

This response is an attempt by the manager to deal with Allan's problem with the computer without investing any of his own time in discovering why Allan is having trouble. The response ignores the problem with coworkers and may aggravate it by making one of them take time to help Allan.

5. "Why do you think the other employees won't help you?"

This response is a probe to learn more about Allan's perceptions about coworkers. However, it assumes that Allan knows the reason for the problem and can describe it, which may not be the case.

6. "You feel that the other employees in the office don't pay any attention to you?"

This response is a restatement to encourage Allan to say more. However, there is no guarantee that it will elicit further comment by Allan.

Part 2

1. "It's been a rough day for you, Jane, but that claims report still has to be completed today."

This response begins by expressing a little sympathy, but the immediate shift of focus to the report makes the speaker appear not to have any real concern for Jane's feelings.

2. "You think that's bad. Let me tell you what happened to me yesterday."

This response shows no sympathy or concern about Jane's feelings, and it ignores the problem of the report. Personal problems are treated as a game of one-upmanship, or who has the worst story to tell.

3. "Jane, we need to talk about the schedule for testing the new software."

This response ignores what Jane just said and arbitrarily changes the subject (fails to synchronize interaction). The response disregards Jane's feelings and the report.

4. "You can't let these things get you down. Just try to forget about it and concentrate on your work."

This response dismisses Jane's feelings in a way that makes her appear inferior. The response shows little sympathy for Jane, and the problem of the report is not directly addressed.

5. "You must be really upset, Jane!"

This is a reflective statement that shows empathy for Jane's feelings, especially if made in a sincere, concerned manner. It is a good initial response, and it invites Jane to say more if she desires. However, it does not directly address the problem of the report.

6. "Is there something I can do to help you with the report?"

This response shows concern for the task but not Jane's feelings. It is inappropriate as an initial response, but after showing concern and sympathy for Jane, it is a good followup response.

Test Bank

Description of Test Bank

This test bank consists of 254 multiple-choice items grouped by chapter and topic. Roughly half of the items are new, and the remainder are from the test bank used with the second edition of the book. There are from 10 to 20 items per chapter. The items measure specific knowledge about the concepts, theories, research findings, and action guidelines discussed in the third edition. Most of the items deal with major concepts and issues rather than with trivial or obscure points. Nevertheless, the items are not intended to measure the ability to evaluate, synthesize, or integrate the material. To assess this type of knowledge, it is necessary to supplement the objective exams with other measures such as essay exams and papers. The review questions at the end of each chapter provide one source of potential essay questions, and they also provide guidance to students in studying for multiple choice exams. Students who take the time to develop answers for the review questions should be able to answer most of the test bank items correctly.

When giving instructions for a test drawn from this set of items, remind students to read each item carefully and examine each response choice before selecting the best one. Careless reading is a common source of error in this type of exam. Tell students to notice when an item is worded negatively (e.g., "Which of the following is not correct?"). Because many of the items are complex, it is important to allow students enough time to read them carefully. When giving a test composed of these items, allow an average of one minute per item.

The test bank is designed to have content validity (representative sampling of key points in the chapters). I tried to avoid common weaknesses in multiple choice items, such as answers that are obvious without reading the book, items that point out the answer to subsequent items, biased distribution of the correct responses, and use of confusing formats such as "all of the above." Most of the items retained from the earlier test bank have strong item statistics (weak items were discarded or revised). Most of the new items have not been pretested, however, and it is advisable to conduct your own item analysis when using them to see if there are any weak items that should be dropped.

The following practices for administration of the test greatly reduce the chance that exam security will be compromised.

• Keep copies of exams in a secure, locked file or cabinet when stored at school.

• If you carry the manual to class regularly to use the case notes, you may want to cut out the test bank and keep it in a more secure location. For example, it is a good idea to keep the test bank at home when it is not being used.

• Pass out tests individually to each student, rather than giving batches of tests to be passed across a row from student to student.

• Ask each student to sign the exam upon receiving it, and tell students they will be held accountable for returning it with their answer sheet.

• If you review the exam in class or allow students to see their results in your office, do not allow students to copy items or keep the exam.

• Vary the content of exams from one term to another so that there is no incentive for students to build a test file on your exams.

Chapter 1: The Nature of Leadership

1. The reason for so many different definitions of leadership is:

   a. scholarly nitpicking
   b. disagreement about what should be considered leadership processes
   c. the fact that leadership behavior is not objectively measurable
   d. the fact that leadership is such a recent topic

2. Definitions of leadership:

   a. strongly influence the design and interpretation of research
   b. are strongly influenced by research on unconscious processes
   c. reflect general agreement about the nature of leadership
   d. are pointless because there is no basis for verification

3. Leadership is essentially:

   a. an authority relationship
   b. an influence process
   c. the ability to make good decisions
   d. an attribution made by followers

4. Leadership effectiveness is best assessed:

   a. by a single objective indicator of group performance
   b. by subordinate evaluations of the leader
   c. by a variety of subjective and objective criteria
   d. by a composite index based on several objective indicators of group performance

5. Which of the following is an indirect effect of leadership?

   a. increase motivation by giving an inspiring speech
   b. increase quality by influencing the culture
   c. increase ability by providing instruction in how to do the task
   d. increase efficiency by coordinating the work

6. Which of the following is not a primary responsibility of leaders according to open systems theory?

   a. avoiding incompatible demands from stakeholders
   b. adapting to the environment
   c. maintaining member commitment and cooperation
   d. organizing and coordinating operations to achieve efficiency

7. Research on leadership has been characterized by:

   a. an integrative orientation
   b. systematic investigation
   c. a diversity of measurement methods within individual studies
   d. a disparity of approaches

141

8. A primary responsibility of top level leadership is to achieve an optimal balance between all but which one of the following?

   a. efficiency and flexibility
   b. task and human relations concerns
   c. prosperity and decline
   d. interests of internal and external stakeholders

9. Participative leadership is best viewed as a combination of which two approaches for studying leadership?

   a. trait and behavior
   b. power-influence and trait
   c. behavior and power-influence
   d. trait and situational

10. Convergence of findings from different research approaches in leadership:

   a. has been a prime concern of most leadership theorists
   b. has been extensively validated by empirical research
   c. is entirely a matter of speculation
   d. is facilitated by an integrating conceptual framework

Chapter 2: The Nature of Managerial Work

1. Research on managerial activities found that managers typically spend the most time:

   a. in their office
   b. with subordinates
   c. reading and writing reports, memos, and correspondence
   d. in informal meetings

2. Which of the following was not found by Mintzberg to be characteristic of managers?

   a. they spend much of their time engaged in oral communication
   b. they spend considerable time engaged in reflective activities such as planning
   c. they spend considerable time engaged in lateral communication
   d. they are engaged in a large variety of brief activities during a typical workday

3. Which was not found by descriptive research on managerial activities?

   a. the content of managerial work is varied and fragmented
   b. the pace of managerial work is hectic and unrelenting
   c. interactions typically involve the exchange of written messages and memos
   d. many interactions involve peers or outsiders

4. The descriptive research found that a network of contacts and cooperative relationships is especially important to:

   a. implement change
   b. motivate subordinates
   c. improve time management
   d. identify quality problems in the work

5. Which was not found by descriptive research on decision processes in organizations?

   a. major decisions are made in an orderly, rational manner
   b. decision processes are prolonged for important decisions
   c. decision processes are highly political
   d. major decisions may result from a series of small, incremental choices

6. Planning in organizations is usually:

   a. formal and detailed
   b. formal and flexible
   d. informal and flexible
   c. informal and detailed

7. Research shows that effective managers:

   a. carefully study each option before acting
   b. experiment with innovative ideas and approaches
   c. get authorization for actions to protect themselves
   d. get complete agreement from all concerned parties before taking action

8. Mintzberg's managerial roles are an attempt to classify descriptions of managerial behavior obtained from:

   a. observation of the managers by researchers
   b. self-report questionnaires filled out by the managers
   c. questionnaires filled out by the subordinates of the managers
   d. interviews with the managers conducted by researchers

9. Which of the following is not one of Mintzberg's three general categories of managerial work?

   a. strategic planning
   b. information processing
   c. decision making
   d. interpersonal behavior

10. Which of Mintzberg's managerial roles usually has the highest priority for managers?

   a. resource allocator
   b. negotiator
   c. disturbance handler
   d. liaison

11. According to Stewart, which of the following statements is <u>not</u> correct?

a. core demands are essentially the same for most managerial jobs
b. constraints depend in part on manager perceptions
c. demands are perceived role expectations
d. managerial behavior is strongly influenced by demands and constraints

12. Which of the following statements about managerial dependence on the situation is correct according to Rosemary Stewart?

a. external demands are less when a manager deals with many outsiders for short periods of time
b. demands by subordinates are greater when they work alone on separate tasks
c. demands by peers are greater when work units are highly inter-dependent
d. demands by superiors are less when the organization is highly centralized

13. Managers in large units tend to:

a. use less delegation
b. use more group decision making
c. spend more time planning and coordinating
d. provide more coaching

14. In comparison to first-line supervisors, executives typically:

a. are more autocratic in making decisions
b. spend less time performing the disturbance handler role
c. are less involved in planning
d. have shorter, more fragmented activities

15. In large units, as compared to small ones:

a. the leader depends less on subordinates to initiate action
b. good performance by subordinates is less likely to be rewarded
c. there is a reduction in the administrative workload
d. there is less need for the leader to manage conflict among factions

16. Less time and skill are needed to manage subordinates who:

a. change tasks frequently
b. have high exposure tasks
c. have variable workloads
d. have tasks with reliable performance indicators

17. In a hostile environment, effective leaders are likely to:

a. consult with subordinates
b. reduce their exposure
c. act more considerate
d. act decisive

18. Which was <u>not</u> mentioned as one of the four general processes in managerial work?

    a. making decisions
    <u>b</u>. evaluating subordinates
    c. developing relationships
    d. influencing people

19. Which of the following was <u>not</u> presented as a guideline for managers?

    a. expand the range of choices
    b. make time for reflective planning
    <u>c</u>. concentrate on reacting to demands
    d. understand reasons for demands and constraints

Chapter 3:   Perspectives on Effective Leadership Behavior

1. A manager who takes time to listen to subordinates, expresses trust in them, and helps them with personal problems is best described as high on:

    a. participative leadership
    <u>b</u>. consideration
    c. initiating structure
    d. consideration and participative leadership

2. Which of the following is <u>not</u> an example of Initiating Structure as defined in the Ohio State studies?

    a. letting subordinates know what is expected of them
    b. criticizing poor work
    <u>c</u>. rewarding subordinates for effective performance
    d. coordinating the activities of subordinates

3. Which of the following kinds of behaviors is <u>not</u> an example of Consideration as defined in the Ohio State Studies?

    a. being friendly and supportive to subordinates
    b. consulting with subordinates on matters of importance to them
    <u>c</u>. providing coaching to subordinates who need to improve their performance
    d. being willing to listen to subordinate problems

4. Fleishman and Harris found that grievances and turnover were lowest when:

    a. Consideration and Initiating Structure were both high
    b. Consideration and Initiating Structure were both low
    <u>c</u>. Consideration was high and Initiating Structure was low
    d. Consideration was low and Initiating Structure was high

5. Which of the following results was found in the early Michigan leadership studies?

   a. effective supervisors spent much of their time working on the task with subordinates
   b. effective supervisors used close supervision to insure the work was done correctly
   c. effective supervisors were careful not to get too friendly with their subordinates
   d. effective supervisors devoted more time to managerial functions such as planning, coordination, and work facilitation

6. A unique contribution of the research by Bowers and Seashore was:

   a. use of field experiments to study leadership effectiveness
   b. measurement of peer leadership as well as supervisory leadership
   c. emphasis on leadership skills rather than leadership behavior
   d. use of observers to measure leader behavior instead of subordinates

7. Which was not a major weakness in most of the questionnaire studies of leadership behavior?

   a. focus was on broad categories of behavior rather than specific behaviors
   b. behavior ratings were biased by stereotypes and attributions
   c. causality was indeterminate due to use of correlation designs
   d. samples of leaders were unrepresentative because most studies used students

8. Most critical incidents studies of leaders find all except which of the following?

   a. respondents are very critical of their leader
   b. establishing effective relations with others is an important behavior category
   c. many reported incidents are specific to the situation
   d. planning is an important category of leader behavior

9. According to Blake and Mouton, effective leaders:

   a. have a high concern for the task and a moderate concern for relationships
   b. have a moderate concern for efficiency, and a high concern for relationships
   c. have a high concern for both efficiency and flexibility
   d. have a high concern for both the task and relationships

10. In the multiplicative version of the high-high theory of leadership effectiveness:

   a. task behavior is more beneficial when relationship behavior is low
   b. task behavior is more beneficial when relationship behavior is high
   c. effects of task behavior and relationship behavior are independent
   d. leaders use the same amount of task and relationship behavior

11. What is the best conclusion from research on the high-high theory of leadership?

   a. the research provides strong support for the additive model
   b. the research provides strong support for the multiplicative model
   c. the research provides strong support for both models
   d. the research fails to provide strong support for either model

12. According to the universal two-factor theory of leadership, an effective leader would be most likely to:

    a. consult with people about how to improve working conditions
    <u>b</u>. consult with people about ways to improve productivity
    c. ask people for small improvements in performance
    d. pressure people to do more work

13. Which was <u>not</u> mentioned as a reason for differences among behavior taxonomies?

    <u>a</u>. credibility of theorist
    b. method of development
    c. level of abstraction
    d. purpose of taxonomy

14. Which is <u>not</u> a method for developing behavior taxonomies?

    <u>a</u>. distributive aggregation
    b. judgmental classification
    c. factor analysis
    d. theoretical-deductive approach

15. Which of the following is <u>not</u> a behavior category in the Yukl integrating taxonomy?

    <u>a</u>. initiating structure
    b. informing
    c. recognizing
    d. planning and organizing

16. Which of the following guidelines was <u>not</u> recommended for improving leadership effectiveness?

    <u>a</u>. concentrate on one concern (facilitate task or improve relationships) at a time
    b. let your behavior be guided by your objectives, priorities, and implicit agendas
    c. select specific forms of behavior that are appropriate for the immediate situation
    d. learn to differentiate among specific managerial practices and use them skillfully

Chapter 4: Specific Behaviors for Managing the Work

1. Which statement about action planning is <u>most</u> accurate?

    a. informal agendas are just as useful as a formal plan for a complex project
    b. most managers prefer to do formal planning rather than spending time solving immediate problems
    <u>c</u>. a short activity list with rough time estimates is appropriate for many simple projects
    d. the more complex and detailed an action plan is, the better it is likely to be

2. What is <u>least</u> likely to be improved by a manager's action planning?

    a. coordination among people working on different parts of a project
    <u>b.</u> development of skills by people working on a project
    c. monitoring of progress on a project
    d. delegation of responsibility for parts of a project

3. Which of the following aspects of action planning is <u>not</u> necessary to develop an event calendar or milestone chart?

    a. identify the optimal sequence of action steps
    <u>b.</u> determine accountability for each action step
    c. determine start times and deadlines for each action step
    d. estimate the time needed to carry out each action step

4. Which remedy was <u>not</u> recommended for action planning when commitment is in doubt for the person who would normally carry out an action step?

    <u>a.</u> reduce the amount of slack in the schedule
    b. monitor the person more closely
    c. try to find a backup person
    d. use influence tactics to increase commitment

5. Effective managers are most likely to:

    a. concentrate on solving easy problems and put off most of the difficult ones
    b. concentrate on solving the most difficult problems and ignore the easy ones
    <u>c.</u> take responsibility for resolving difficult but important problems
    d. form a committee to study a difficult problem

6. When solving a problem, effective managers are <u>less</u> likely to:

    <u>a.</u> deal with each problem separately as soon as it is discovered
    b. make a quick but systematic diagnosis of the cause of the problem
    c. experiment with innovative solutions
    d. take decisive action to deal with a problem that has become a crisis

7. Compared to planning, most problem solving by managers:

    a. is more proactive
    b. is more rational
    <u>c.</u> has a shorter time perspective
    <u>d.</u> takes longer to complete

8. Less clarifying behavior is needed by a manager when:

    <u>a.</u> the task of subordinates is highly structured and repetitive
    b. the task is performed by subordinates with little prior experience
    c. the task requires continuous coordination among subordinates
    d. the task has multiple performance criteria with tradeoffs among them

9. When subordinates have a high level of role ambiguity, a manager should use more:

    a. informing
    b. problem solving
    c. clarifying
    d. monitoring

10. What approach should a manager use to set performance goals for subordinates?

    a. set a goal to "do your best" on each important aspect of the job
    b. set specific goals that are easy to achieve to maintain subordinate confidence
    c. set challenging goals that stretch subordinates
    d. set goals that are specific and challenging

11. When assigning non-routine tasks, effective managers are least likely to:

    a. assign several tasks at the same time
    b. use clear, easy language to explain what needs to be done
    c. explain the reasons for the assignment
    d. check for understanding of the assignment

12. The recommended way to provide instruction in how to do a complex procedure with several sequential steps is first to explain and demonstrate each step, then:

    a. have the person do each step silently while you observe it
    b. have the person recite each step before doing it
    c. have the person recite each step before you do it, then have the person explain each step as he or she does it for you
    d. have the person recite the entire sequence of steps, then have the person do the entire sequence of steps silently while you observe

13. When informing subordinates, effective managers are least likely to:

    a. talk to subordinates to find out what information they need
    b. arrange for subordinates to have direct access to key information sources
    c. highlight important information for subordinates
    d. pass on copies of all written materials such as memos and reports

14. In a crisis situation involving an external threat (e.g., hostile action by enemies, disruption of operations due to shortages or a natural disaster) it is usually best to:

    a. tell subordinates that the problem is not serious so they will not worry about it
    b. explain the nature of the crisis and ask people to trust you to deal with it
    c. hold lengthy meetings with subordinates to talk about the crisis and decide what to do about it
    d. explain the crisis, describe what is being done about it, and provide periodic briefings

15. When monitoring internal operations, effective managers are <u>least</u> likely to:

    a. identify and measure key indicators of performance outcomes
    <u>b</u>. have subordinates prepare detailed written reports on a weekly basis
    c. measure key process variables as well as outcomes
    d. develop independent sources of information

16. Which of the following is <u>least</u> likely to improve the effectiveness of internal monitoring by a manager in charge of several widely-dispersed work sites?

    a. visit the work sites frequently
    <u>b</u>. give advance notice of visits so subordinates will be prepared
    c. walk around to observe operations and talk to employees
    d. ask specific, open-ended questions about the work

17. Which of the following is <u>least</u> likely to be a benefit of progress review meetings?

    a. evaluate whether the manager's goals and action plans are realistic
    <u>b</u>. prevent a subordinate from making any mistakes
    c. coordinate the activities of different subordinates
    d. evaluate whether the subordinate's goals and action plans are realistic

18. Less monitoring by a manager is necessary when subordinates have:

    <u>a</u>. tasks that are short and highly structured
    b. interdependent tasks requiring close coordination
    c. projects that are long and complex
    d. tasks for which mistakes are costly

19. Which is the best guideline for scheduling progress review meetings?

    a. they should be held at least once every week
    b. they should be held infrequently to avoid wasting time
    c. they should be held more often for tasks which take a long time to complete
    <u>d</u>. they should be held more often for important, sensitive tasks

20. Which of the following was <u>not</u> given as a guideline for external monitoring?

    a. examine a wide range of developments and trends in the environment
    b. make an extra effort to learn what clients and customers want and need
    c. identify both the strengths and weaknesses of competing products
    <u>d</u>. analyze the environment by yourself and rely on your own intuition

1.   Which of the following is <u>not</u> an example of supporting behavior, as defined by Yukl?

   a.   back up a subordinate who is right in a dispute with higher management
   <u>b</u>.   give an award to a subordinate who set a new sales record
   c.   remember details about a subordinate's interests and family
   d.   help a subordinate with a personal problem

2.   Which of the following was recommended for facilitating supportive communication?

   a.   use dramatic gestures
   b.   use judgmental responses
   <u>c</u>.   synchronize interaction
   d.   exploit preconceptions

3.   Which of the following is <u>not</u> a technique for active listening?

   a.   reflection of feelings
   b.   restatement
   <u>c</u>.   projection of feelings
   d.   probing questions

4.   Which of the following was <u>not</u> recommended for effective coaching?

   a.   use concrete examples, diagrams, and mnemonics in explanations
   b.   relate specific training objectives to the person's interests and career ambitions
   <u>c</u>.   integrate complex material into longer learning modules
   d.   allow ample opportunity for practice with feedback

5.   Which was <u>not</u> recommended for developing a subordinate's managerial planning skills ?

   <u>a</u>.   assign a challenging task with detailed instructions in how to do it
   b.   encourage and facilitate attendance at relevant training programs
   c.   serve as a role model by displaying effective planning behavior
   d.   involve the subordinate in planning and decision making for the work unit

6.   Which of the following was <u>not</u> recommended for recognizing?

   <u>a</u>.   recognize only performance that is outstanding
   b.   spend some time each day looking for effective behavior to recognize
   c.   give people in support jobs as much recognition as people in high visibility jobs
   d.   recognize a variety of contributions and achievements

7.   Which of the following was <u>not</u> recommended for giving praise?

   a.   be specific and explain why the person's behavior was effective
   b.   give praise soon after the behavior occurs
   <u>c</u>.   give praise in private
   d.   be sincere

151

8. Rewards are <u>less</u> likely to be effective in reinforcing behavior if they are:

    a. spontaneous
    b. immediate
    c. based on clear standards
    <u>d</u>. intangible

9. Conflict is most likely to occur between two people with:

    a. independent tasks and similar goals
    b. independent tasks and different goals
    c. interdependent tasks and similar goals
    <u>d</u>. interdependent tasks and different goals

10. Persuasive appeals are most likely to be effective for resolving a conflict between two people when:

    a. they understand each other's position
    <u>b</u>. they have compatible goals
    c. they have equal status
    d. the issue is important to both of them

11. What is the best approach for handling conflict when there is little hostility or distrust?

    a. persuasion
    b. bargaining
    c. accommodation
    <u>d</u>. integrative problem solving

12. Which of the following is most likely to occur in integrative problem solving?

    a. positional commitments are made by both parties
    b. both parties agree on a split-the-difference compromise
    c. specific demands are made for each issue
    <u>d</u>. information about needs and priorities is disclosed

13. Which of the following was <u>not</u> recommended for integrative problem solving?

    a. use joint fact finding and problem definition
    b. state problems in terms of specifics rather than abstract principles
    c. develop a range of solutions acceptable to both parties
    <u>d</u>. negotiate each issue separately

14. Which of the following was <u>not</u> recommended as a process consultation procedure?

    <u>a</u>. provide more support and assistance to the weaker party
    b. discourage threats, exaggeration, and stereotyping
    c. use humor to reduce tension
    d. encourage restatement of the other party's position

15. Which of the following was <u>not</u> recommended for effective teambuilding by managers?

    <u>a</u>. introduce competition among members of the group to make the work more interesting
    b. use ceremonies and rituals to celebrate group achievements and traditional values
    c. use symbols such as slogans, emblems, and uniforms to build identification with the group
    d. emphasize common interests and shared objectives

16. What is <u>least</u> important as a reason for managers to develop a large network of contacts?

    a. to facilitate a manager's career advancement
    <u>b</u>. to satisfy a high need for affiliation
    c. to obtain information about the external environment
    d. to gain assistance and political support

17. Which of the following was <u>not</u> recommended for maintaining an effective network?

    a. increase mutual dependency with people you want to keep in your network
    <u>b</u>. avoid doing a favor for anyone who does not agree to return the favor
    c. show appreciation for favors done for you by people
    d. use ingratiation with network members

Chapter 6 Participative Leadership and Delegation

1. The decision procedure that gives a subordinate the most influence is:

    a. autocratic decision-making
    b. joint decision-making
    c. consultation
    <u>d</u>. delegation

2. Which statement about participation research is most accurate?

    a. there has been little research on the consequences of participation
    b. participation usually results in better subordinate performance
    <u>c</u>. results from the participation research are inconsistent
    d. most participation research was conducted with undergraduates

3. Participation is most likely to result in:

    a. faster decisions
    b. better decisions
    c. consensus decisions
    <u>d</u>. greater decision acceptance

4. In the Vroom-Yetton model of decision participation, the rules for determining the appropriate decision procedures protect:

    a. the leader's responsibility for the decision and authority to implement it
    b. subordinate rights to self-determination in the choice of jobs
    c. subordinate rights to be consulted about decisions affecting them
    d. the quality and acceptance of the decision

5. According to the Vroom and Yetton model of leadership, the leader should not make an autocratic decision when:

    a. the quality of the decision is important
    b. subordinate acceptance of the decision is important
    c. decision quality is important and subordinates have relevant information
    d. subordinate acceptance and decision quality are both important

6. In what important way does the Vroom-Yetton model differ from earlier participation theory?

    a. decision making is described as a sequential process that may involve different decision procedures
    b. decision procedures are described on a continuum, from autocratic decisions to group decisions
    c. the feasible set of decision procedures for a particular situation is identified
    d. the skills necessary for effective participation are identified

7. According to the Vroom and Yetton model of leadership, the leader should not use group decision-making when:

    a. the goals of subordinates are inconsistent with organizational objectives
    b. the leader knows the best solution to the problem
    c. the quality of the decision is important
    d. subordinates are likely to disagree with each other about the best solution

8. Which of the following was not recommended as a guideline for participative leadership?

    a. present a proposal as tentative and encourage people to improve it
    b. quickly dismiss ideas with obvious weaknesses
    c. let people know how their ideas and suggestions were used
    d. restate ideas and concerns expressed by someone to verify understanding

9. Consultation is more effective than group decisions when:

    a. subordinates disagree with each other about the best course of action
    b. the manager must decide how to respond to an immediate crisis
    c. the manager has little personal power
    d. subordinates share the manager's goals

10. Which of the following is least likely to be a benefit from using delegation?

   a. less responsibility for the manager
   b. increased subordinate job commitment
   c. development of subordinate skills
   d. efficient time management for the manager

11. What is least likely to be a reason for failure to delegate authority to a subordinate?

   a. the manager is confident and secure
   b. the manager has a high need for power
   c. subordinate jobs are highly interdependent
   d. there is high standardization of procedures

12. A manager should not delegate tasks that are:

   a. unpleasant
   b. symbolically important
   c. complex and difficult
   d. urgent but not important

13. Which of the following was not a guideline for how to delegate effectively?

   a. specify the subordinate's scope of authority and limits of discretion
   b. explain the new responsibilities and the expected results
   c. arrange for the subordinate to receive relevant information
   d. tell the subordinate to report any problems immediately

14. For a manager who is overloaded, the most appropriate tasks to delegate are:

   a. low priority tasks that are not urgent
   b. low priority tasks that are urgent
   c. high priority tasks that are not urgent
   d. high priority tasks that are urgent

15. What is the best reaction when a subordinate makes a mistake for the first time in a delegated task?

   a. point out the mistake and warn the subordinate not to do it again.
   b. provide detailed instructions about the proper way to do the task
   c. discuss the reasons for the mistake and how it can be avoided in the future
   d. ignore the mistake this time but monitor the subordinate more closely in the future

16. According to Hackman, self managed groups are least likely to be successful when:

   a. they are allowed to determine their own objectives and priorities
   b. they have a distinctive and important task that requires cooperation and teamwork
   c. they are allowed to organize themselves without interference from the company or the union
   d. they have complete access to information about their work, including productivity, quality, revenues, costs, and profits.

17. What is the most useful role for the external leader of a self-managed group?

    a. leave the group alone to do its thing without any interference
    d. monitor the group closely to ensure it does not become a social club
    b. select the internal leader and select new members when they are needed
    <u>d</u>. serve as a coach, facilitator, and advocate for the group

Chapter 7: Sources of Power and Influence

1. Authority is:

    a. a consequence of power
    b. a source of power
    <u>c</u>. both a source and consequence of power
    d. neither a source nor a consequence of power

2. The primary determinant of a manager's power over someone is:

    a. the manager's expertise in relation to that of the other person
    b. the relative status of the manager and other person
    <u>c</u>. dependence of the other person on the manager
    d. the other person's counterpower

3. Which of the following was <u>not</u> given as an example of resistance behavior?

    <u>a</u>. act indifferent while carrying out a request
    b. delay acting
    c. make excuses
    d. appeal to higher authorities

4. Acting charming and considerate is most likely to increase a person's:

    a. expert power
    <u>b</u>. referent power
    c. legitimate power
    d. reward power

5. A leader's credibility affects his or her:

    a. reward power
    b. expert power
    c. reward and expert power
    <u>d</u>. reward, expert, and coercive power

6. Which of the following is <u>not</u> recommended as a way to increase your expert power?

    <u>a</u>. show others how to solve problems for themselves
    b. avoid making rash or careless statements
    c. act confident and decisive in a crisis
    d. develop exclusive sources of technical information

7. Which type of power is most dependent upon loyalty and friendship toward the person attempting to exercise power?

   a. charismatic power
   <u>b</u>. referent power
   c. expert power
   d. counterpower

8. A leader's position power is determined by all except which of the following?

   a. legitimate authority
   <u>b</u>. relevant expertise
   c. control over rewards
   d. control over information

9. The coercive power of managers:

   a. is greater over peers than over subordinates
   <u>b</u>. is less than it was in earlier times
   c. is greater for lower-level managers than for executives
   d. cannot be used to any advantage

10. Control over information sources gives a manager power over:

    a. subordinates
    b. subordinates and peers
    c. peers and superiors
    <u>d</u>. peers, superiors, and subordinates

11. Coercive power:

    a. is seldom used by managers
    b. invariably results in punishment
    <u>c</u>. improves performance in some situations
    d. is highly effective when used with subordinates

12. Which two kinds of power have been found to be related most strongly to leader effectiveness in achieving a high level of group performance?

    <u>a</u>. referent and expert power
    b. reward and legitimate power
    c. referent and legitimate power
    d. reward and expert power

13. Which two types of power are most likely to result in subordinate compliance rather than commitment or resistance?

    a. reward and expert power
    <u>b</u>. reward and legitimate power
    c. expert and legitimate power
    d. expert and referent power

14. Which influence process is most likely to result in continued commitment regardless of the agent's subsequent actions?

    a. instrumental compliance
    b. personal identification
    c. compliance with authority
    d. internalization

15. The status and influence accorded an emergent leader by followers is primarily determined by the leader's:

    a. social popularity
    b. seniority in the group
    c. control over rewards
    d. demonstrated competence and loyalty

16. If a leader's innovative proposal leads to failure, under what conditions will the group's evaluation of the leader be the most unfavorable?

    a. the leader made unrealistic assumptions
    b. the leader failed to anticipate the actions of competitors or enemies
    c. the leader exercised poor judgment when implementing the proposal
    d. the leader pursued his or her own selfish interests

17. Which of the following is not one of the three determinant's of subunit power specified by strategic contingencies theory?

    a. political skill
    b. expertise in solving problems
    c. centrality in the workflow
    d. uniqueness of expertise

18. When a prominent opponent of a policy is induced to accept an administrative position responsible for implementing the policy, this is an example of:

    a. cooptation
    b. coalition formation
    c. symbolic action
    d. institutionalization

19. Which statement about institutionalization in organizations is most accurate?

    a. it describes how subunits with relevant expertise gain power in organizations
    b. it makes it easier for organizations to adapt to a changing environment
    c. it describes how people use power to gain more power
    d. it demonstrates why political tactics are unnecessary to maintain power

20. How much position power and personal power should a leader have to be effective?

    a. maximum position and personal power
    b. maximum position power and moderate personal power
    c. moderate position and personal power
    d. minimal position power and maximum personal power

Chapter 8: Influence Processes and Managerial Effectiveness

1. Asking your boss to help you influence a peer is an example of:

    a. a pressure tactic
    b. a legitimating tactic
    c. a coalition tactic
    d. cooptation

2. Offering to share the benefits from a project if the target agrees to work on it is an example of what type of influence tactic?

    a. inspirational appeal
    b. coalition
    c. exchange
    d. personal appeal

3. Which type of influence tactic is most likely to be used to influence a superior?

    a. rational persuasion
    b. ingratiation tactics
    c. exchange tactics
    d. coalition tactics

4. What influence tactic is used most often in influence attempts with subordinates?

    a. rational persuasion
    b. pressure
    c. consultation
    d. exchange

5. Which statement about objectives of influence attempts in different directions is correct?

    a. attempts to change the way the work is done occur most often in a lateral direction
    b. attempts to get a person to do a task better or faster occur most often in a downward direction
    c. attempts to obtain more resources and political support occur most often in an lateral direction
    d. attempts to obtain personal benefits occur most often in a downward direction

6. Which influence tactic is used more to influence superiors than to influence subordinates?

    a. consultation
    b. coalition
    c. exchange
    d. legitimating

7. Which two influence tactics are more likely to be used in a followup influence attempt than in an initial influence attempt?

    a. exchange and personal appeals
    b. pressure and coalition
    c. personal appeals and legitimating tactics
    d. pressure and rational persuasion

8. Which tactics are most likely to result in resistance?

    a. pressure and exchange
    b. ingratiation and personal appeals
    c. exchange and legitimating tactics
    d. pressure and legitimating tactics

9. Which tactics are most likely to result in target commitment?

    a. rational persuasion and exchange
    b. consultation and personal appeal
    c. inspirational appeal and consultation
    d. exchange and ingratiation

10. Effective managers:

    a. have so much authority that they seldom need to use influence tactics.
    b. use all nine influence tactics frequently in their daily influence attempts
    c. rely on rational persuasion and exchange for most influence attempts
    d. use a mix of influence tactics that vary depending on the situation

11. According to LMX Theory, most leaders:

    a. establish a favorable relationship with each subordinate
    b. establish a special relationship with their boss
    c. are unable to establish a favorable relationship with subordinates
    d. establish a special relationship with a small number of subordinates

12. Which was not found in Graen's research on leader-member exchange?

    a. in-group subordinates performed better than out-group subordinates
    b. effective leaders had highly differentiated in-group and out-group relationships
    c. leaders got more benefits from in-group exchanges than from out-group exchanges
    d. in-group subordinates received more benefits than out-group subordinates

13. When is development of a special exchange relationship with subordinates least likely?

    a. the leader has substantial authority
    b. the leader is overloaded with duties and responsibilities
    c. the leader has an unfavorable relationship with superiors
    d. the leader has many immediate subordinates

14. When is a manager most likely to attribute poor performance to lack of subordinate effort or ability?

    a. the subordinate has made excuses and denied responsibility
    b. the poor performance has serious consequences for the work unit
    c. the manager is dependent on the subordinate
    d. the subordinate performs other types of tasks effectively

15. Studies on how managers perceive poor performance by a subordinate find that:

    a. managers are biased toward attributing the cause to internal factors such as lack of motivation or ability
    b. managers are biased toward attributing the cause to bad luck (unforeseen random events)
    c. managers are biased toward attributing the cause to external factors such as insufficient resources or lack of cooperation by others
    d. most managers make an accurate attribution about the cause of poor performance by a subordinate

16. Which is the least likely response by a manager who attributes the cause of poor performance to a subordinate's lack of motivation?

    a. more coaching
    b. warnings or a reprimand
    c. closer monitoring
    d. new incentives

17. Which of the following behaviors was not recommended for using legitimate power?

    a. verify the legitimacy of questionable requests
    b. expand your scope of authority over all aspects of the work
    c. insist on compliance when appropriate
    d. follow up to verify compliance

18. Which of the following is a recommended guideline for disciplinary action?

    a. a first offense should be ignored because the person is usually just seeking attention
    b. the same disciplinary action should be taken after every offense to appear consistent
    c. each offense should be followed by the strongest possible disciplinary action to discourage additional offenses
    d. disciplinary action should begin with an oral warning and be progressively increased with each additional offense

19. Which pair of tactics are recommended ways to use referent power?

    a. role modeling and personal appeal
    b. personal appeal and polite request
    c. role modeling and image management
    d. personal appeal and image management

20. Which was not recommended as a guideline for using expert power?

    a. act confident and decisive
    b. explain the reasons for a request
    c. make a persuasive proposal based on logic and technical information
    d. overwhelm someone who questions your judgment with a barrage of supporting facts

Chapter 9: Managerial Traits and Skills

1. Which trait is least likely to be found in effective managers?

    a. internal locus of control orientation
    b. integrity
    c. defensiveness
    d. emotional stability

2. What was not found in the longitudinal study of managerial assessment at AT&T?

    a. advancement was faster if a manager was given easy, routine assignments the first few years
    b. advancement was faster for managers with strong oral communication skill
    c. advancement was faster for managers with strong ambition to advance
    d. advancement twenty years later was predicted by assessment center scores obtained in the first year

3. In the study of managerial assessment at AT&T, what type of skill was least useful for predicting rate of advancement twenty years later?

    a. technical skill
    b. interpersonal skill
    c. cognitive skill
    d. administrative skill

4. Which of the following traits did Miner find was least important for managerial success?

    a. desire to exercise power
    b. willingness to do routine administrative paperwork
    c. desire to compete with peers
    d. positive attitude toward authority figures

5. How were motives measured in McClelland's research on managerial motivation?

    a. motive questionnaire
    b. projective test
    c. written test of manifest needs
    d. coded interviews

6. What pattern of need priorities (from strongest need to weakest) is most common in effective managers?

    a. power, achievement, affiliation
    b. achievement, power, affiliation
    c. power, affiliation, achievement
    d. achievement, affiliation, power

7. McClelland found that the dominant need in entrepreneurial managers was:

    a. esteem
    b. affiliation
    c. power
    d. achievement

8. Research at the Center for Creative Leadership found that in comparison to managers who derailed in their career, managers who continued to be successful had more:

    a. ambition to succeed
    b. technical brilliance
    c. interpersonal skill
    d. self confidence

9. Research at CCL found that leaders who derailed in their careers:

    a. experienced a string of successes in their earlier managerial positions
    b. developed many cooperative relationships in their earlier positions
    c. had early experience in a variety of different types of managerial positions
    d. had experience with earlier positions that were very difficult and stressful

10. In comparison to a person with a personalized power concern, a person with a socialized power concern is more likely to:

    a. make decisions alone
    b. socialize frequently with subordinates
    c. inspire loyalty among subordinates
    d. make subordinates feel strong and responsible

11. What conclusion about self confidence is most accurate:

    a. self confidence is unimportant when you have enough power to get things done
    b. the more self confidence a leader has, the more effective the leader will be
    c. moderately high self confidence is probably optimal for most situations
    d. the leader does not need to be confident as long as he or she appears confident

12. A manager's ability to maintain cooperative relationships with people is likely to depend the most on which of the following traits?

    a. need for affiliation
    b. emotional maturity
    c. internal control orientation
    d. self confidence

13. Extremely narcissistic leaders are least likely to:

    a. perceive human relationships in simplistic terms
    b. seek objective advice from subordinates and peers
    c. undertake ambitious projects to glorify themselves
    d. become preoccupied with their own power and prestige

14. What is the most accurate conclusion about traits and success as a manager?

    a. managers with a strong personalized power orientation are seldom effective
    b. managers with a strong socialized power orientation are usually effective
    c. managers with a strong socialized power orientation are more likely to be effective than managers with a strong personalized power orientation
    d. managers with strong power motivation are usually effective, regardless of which type of orientation they have

15. Which pattern of skills is most likely to be associated with effective leadership?

    a. technical and interpersonal skills
    b. technical and conceptual skills
    c. conceptual and interpersonal skills
    d. technical, conceptual, and interpersonal skills

16. In comparison to first-line supervisors, top executives usually need:

    a. more interpersonal skill, and less technical skill
    b. more conceptual skill, and less technical skill
    c. more interpersonal skill, and less conceptual skill
    d. more technical skill, and less interpersonal skill

17. What type of skills are least likely to transfer from one type of managerial position to another?

    a. interpersonal
    b. administrative
    c. technical
    d. conceptual

18. According to Jacobs and Jacques, what time perspective should top executives have in their strategic planning for future events?

    a. 2 - 3 years
    b. 3 - 5 years
    c. 5 -10 years
    d. 10 - 20 years

19. Which of the following was not presented as a guideline for career planning?

    a. display strengths and hide weaknesses to maintain an image of infallibility
    b. seek information about your strengths and weaknesses and learn from feedback
    c. take advantage of opportunities to develop relevant skills that are deficient
    d. select subordinates with complementary strengths and give them responsibility for aspects of the work they are more qualified to handle

Chapter 10: Situational Theories of Effective Leadership

1. According to the Path-Goal theory of leadership, the effects of leader behavior are moderated by:

    a. leader personality and subordinate characteristics
    b. subordinate characteristics and environmental factors
    c. leader personality and environmental factors
    d. leader personality and skills

2. The central explanatory process in Path-Goal Theory of leadership is:

    a. the influence of leader behavior on subordinate expectations
    b. the influence of leader expectations on subordinate behavior
    c. the influence of leader expectations on subordinate expectations
    d. the influence of leader behavior on group organization

3. According to Path-Goal Theory, directive leadership is most effective when:

    a. the task is simple and repetitive
    b. subordinate work roles are ambiguous
    c. relations between the leader and subordinates are good
    d. the task requires a high level of teamwork

4. According to Path-Goal Theory, supportive leadership contributes most to subordinate satisfaction and motivation when the task is:

    a. tedious and stressful
    b. complex and variable
    c. simple and repetitive
    d. interesting and enjoyable

5. Which of the following recommendations is most consistent with Path-Goal Theory?

   a. raise the standards that must be achieved by an employee to earn a bonus
   b. give the same bonus to all employees with the same type of job to ensure equity
   c. reduce the size of bonuses so employees must work harder to earn the same amount
   d. make bonuses contingent on each employee's individual performance

6. According to the Kerr-Jermier theory on substitutes for leadership:

   a. leadership is especially important when it is difficult to find substitutes for employees who quit.
   b. effective leaders use substitutes to fill in for them when they must be absent from the work unit.
   c. leadership is largely redundant when there are many substitutes present in the situation.
   d. successful leaders replace poor performing subordinates with more capable substitutes

7. According to Kerr and Jermier, hierarchical leadership is <u>least</u> important when there are:

   a. few substitutes and neutralizers
   b. few substitutes and many neutralizers
   c. many substitutes and few neutralizers
   d. many substitutes and neutralizers

8. Which of the following conditions is <u>not</u> a substitute for instrumental or directive leadership according to Kerr and Jermier?

   a. high subordinate expertise
   b. high task structure
   c. high formalization
   d. high position power

9. Which of the following conditions is <u>not</u> a substitute for supportive leadership?

   a. intrinsically satisfying task
   b. cohesive work group
   c. professional orientation of employees
   d. clear rules and standards

10. According to Yukl's Multiple Linkage Model, short-term leader effectiveness depends primarily on what the leader does to:

    a. maximize subordinate motivation
    b. correct any deficiencies in intervening variables
    c. improve planning and coordinating
    d. remove organizational constraints

11. Which of the following is an intervening variable in Yukl's Multiple Linkage Model?

a. subordinate effort and commitment
b. organizational policies
c. leader behavior
d. leader position power

12. According to Yukl's Multiple Linkage Model, a leader's long-term effectiveness depends primarily on:

a. the leader's interpersonal skills
b. the leader's ability to make the situation more favorable
c. the leader's technical skills for problem solving
d. the leader's ability to gain more power over subordinates

13. In comparison to other situational leadership theories, Yukl's Multiple Linkage Model:

a. has more empirical support
b. has more specific propositions about leader effectiveness
c. has more intervening and situational variables
d. is better known

14. Which is not a determinant of situational favorability in the LPC Contingency Theory?

a. task structure
b. group size
c. position power
d. leader-member relations

15. In comparison to a leader with a low LPC score, a high LPC leader:

a. is less critical of coworkers with whom he cannot work effectively
b. is more participative and considerate, regardless of the situation
c. is more concerned with the task than with interpersonal relations
d. is less likely to be effective as a leader

16. According to Fiedler's LPC Contingency Model, a leader with a high LPC score will perform best when the situation:

a. is highly favorable
b. is highly unfavorable
c is moderately favorable
d. is either highly favorable or highly unfavorable

17. According to Fiedler's LPC Contingency Model, when the leadership situation involves either very high or low situational control, effective leaders are likely to have:

a. low LPC scores
b. moderate position power
c. high LPC scores
d. good leader-member relations

18. According to Fiedler's cognitive resource theory, intelligence is least likely to be related to leader effectiveness when there is:

a. a complex, unstructured task
b. a directive leader
c. high interpersonal stress
d. an inexperienced leader

19. According to Cognitive Resource Theory, when there is high interpersonal stress, the best predictor of leader success is the leader's:

a. stress tolerance
b. intelligence
c. experience
d. use of group problem solving

20. Which of the following was recommended for future trait research:

a. focus on linear relationships between individual traits and effectiveness
b. focus on key traits that are inherited
c. look for new, as yet undiscovered, traits
d. examine patterns of traits in relation to behavior and effectiveness

Chapter 11:   Charismatic Leadership

1. According to House, charismatic leaders are not likely to:

a. define work roles in economic terms
b. use impression management
c. arouse follower needs
d. use role modeling

2. According to House, a charismatic leader is most likely to have a high need for:

a. power
b. achievement
c. affiliation
d. esteem

3. According to House, a charismatic leader is likely to:

a. demand only a little, and express confidence that subordinates can do it easily without much effort
b. demand a great deal and talk about how hurt and disappointed he/she will be if subordinates fail to deliver
c. demand a great deal but express doubts that subordinates have the necessary motivation and ability to do it
d. demand a great deal and express confidence that subordinates can do it with a concerted effort

4. According to Bass, charismatic leadership is <u>least</u> likely to be found in:

    a. a new, innovative organization that is prospering
    b. a new, innovative organization that is failing
    <u>c</u>. an old, established organization that is prospering
    d. an old, established organization that is failing

5. According to Conger and Kanungo, attributions of charisma are <u>not</u> likely for a leader who:

    a. creates dissatisfaction with current conditions
    b. makes personal sacrifices to achieve the vision
    <u>c</u>. acts in conventional ways to achieve the vision
    d. recognizes opportunities to make successful changes

6. According to Conger and Kanungo, charismatic leaders are most likely to advocate:

    a. continued loyalty to established values and traditions about how things are done
    b. small, incremental changes in how things are done in the organization
    c. radical changes both in how things are done and in the primary values of followers
    <u>d</u>. major changes that are consistent with the primary values of followers

7. Which behavior is <u>least</u> likely to be used by a charismatic leader according to Shamir, House, and Arthur?

    <u>a</u>. encourage followers to project their guilt and hostility to an external group
    b. tell stories about the group's past successes and heroic deeds
    c. use slogans, rituals, and symbols to give the group a unique identity
    d. use vivid emotional language to articulate a vision of a better future

8. What are the two most important influence processes in the Shamir et al. self-concept theory of charismatic leadership?

    a. personal identification and internalization
    <u>b</u>. internalization and social identification
    c. personal identification and social identification
    d. internalization and instrumental compliance

9. According to Shamir et al., the vision articulated by charismatic leaders emphasizes:

    a. specific and immediate ideological objectives
    b. tangible benefits that justify exceptional follower effort
    <u>c</u>. symbolic and expressive aspects of the work itself
    d. factual evidence about the feasibility of the objectives

10. Follower dependence on the leader and unquestioning obedience is <u>least</u> important in:

    a. Conger and Kanungo's theory of charismatic leadership
    <u>b</u>. Shamir's self concept theory of charismatic leadership
    c. psychoanalytic explanations of charisma
    d. House's theory of charismatic leadership

11. What is the least important aspect of charismatic leadership in Meindl's social contagion theory?

    a. activation of a latent social identity involving heroic action for a righteous cause
    b. arousal of motives within each individual follower by a leader who inspires loyalty and commitment to ideological objectives
    c. attribution of charisma to a leader to rationalize strong emotions and behavior inconsistent with past social identities and espoused beliefs
    d. release of inhibitions and imitation of behavior displayed by other followers

12. In which two theories of charismatic leadership is articulation of an inspiring vision not important for explaining the leader's influence on followers?

    a. Meindl's social contagion theory, and psychoanalytic theory
    b. Shamir's self concept theory, and Conger and Kanungo's attribution theory
    c. Conger and Kanungo's attribution theory, and psychoanalytic theory
    d. Meindl's social contagion theory, and Shamir's self concept theory

13. Descriptive research on narcissistic charismatics found that they are likely to:

    a. pay attention to details and spend the time necessary to guide and facilitate the implementation of their vision in the organization
    b. give recognition to followers who make important contributions to strengthen their loyalty and commitment to the vision
    c. plan carefully for a successor who is qualified to protect the vision and ensure its continuity after the leader departs
    d. become assured that their judgment is infallible and press ahead in a persistent quest to attain their vision

14. What is the least likely reaction of a narcissistic charismatic to information that a plan or strategy devised by the leader is failing?

    a. deny the negative information and emphasize the positive aspects of the plan
    b. urge followers to redouble their effort to make the plan succeed
    c. take responsibility for the failure and learn from it
    d. blame the failure on a subordinate and dismiss the person

15. What conclusion is best supported in the case study by Roberts of a school administrator?

    a. followers attribute charisma to a new leader who uses unconventional behavior and enthusiastic visioning to deal successfully with a crisis
    b. followers attribute charisma to a new leader who uses unconventional behavior and enthusiastic visioning to deal with a crisis, regardless of the outcome
    c. followers attribute charisma to a new leader who uses unconventional behavior and enthusiastic visioning, regardless of whether there is a crisis
    d. charisma is unlikely to be attributed to any new leader in a highly bureaucratic organization, regardless of the situation

16. According to Musser, positive charismatics seek to instill commitment:

    a. only to themselves
    b. only to ideological goals
    c. to themselves more than to ideology
    d. to ideology more than to themselves

Chapter 12: Transformational and Cultural Leadership

1. According to Burns, transforming leaders are most likely to appeal to:

    a. fairness and reciprocity
    b. ideals and moral values
    c. self-interest
    d. respect for rules and tradition

2. According to Burns, which statement about transforming leadership is not correct?

    a. it can involve appeals to greed, jealousy, or hatred
    b. it can involve subordinates influencing superiors
    c. it can occur in the day-to-day acts of ordinary people
    d. it can occur at any level of the organization

3. According to Bass, transformational leaders:

    a. appeal only to positive moral values
    b. exchange rewards for loyalty
    c. rely primarily on rational persuasion
    d. empower followers and activate their higher-order needs

4. Which of the following is not a transformational behavior according to Bass?

    a. individualized consideration
    b. contingent reward behavior
    c. intellectual stimulation
    d. inspirational motivation

5. Which statement about transformational leadership is not correct according to Bass?

    a. charisma is a necessary but not sufficient condition for transformational leadership
    b. transformational leadership has a stronger effect on subordinate performance than transactional leadership
    c. effective leaders use transformational leadership but not transactional leadership
    d. effective leaders use both transformational and transactional leadership

6. According to Schein, organization culture is best described as:

   a. espoused values and objectives of the organization
   b. basic values and beliefs shared by members
   c. member commitment to the organization
   d. member appreciation for the arts, music, and literature

7. What provides a leader the most influence on organization culture according to Schein?

   a. design of organization structure
   b. leader attention and actions
   c. design of the organization's facilities
   d. stories and myths propagated by the leader

8. Which statement about organization culture is not correct according to Schein?

   a. culture helps people maintain comfortable and cooperative relationships within the organization
   b. culture helps people understand how things are done in the organization
   c. culture helps people understand the environment and how to respond to it
   d. culture is easily changed by top management to manipulate and exploit employees

9. The least effective way for a leader to change the organization culture is to:

   a. take dramatic, symbolic actions that emphasize new values or priorities
   b. set an example of appropriate behavior for people to emulate
   c. make formal statements to explain the leader's values and beliefs
   d. redesign the organization structure and management systems to support the leader's vision and strategy

10. According to Tichy and Devanna, a vision is less likely to be successful if:

    a. it is a source of self-esteem for all members, rather than glorifying only the leader
    b. it is a general picture rather than a detailed plan
    c. it is developed by the leader working alone, rather than by a participative process
    d. it is expressed in ideological terms rather than economic terms

11. According to Tichy and Devanna, transformational leaders are likely to:

    a. institute change, then create a vision to justify it
    b. use attitude surveys to identify follower values
    c. persuade followers to make cautious, incremental changes
    d. develop external networks to learn about the organization's strengths and weaknesses

12. Bennis and Nanus found that successful leaders:

    a. developed a vision through a mysterious inner process
    b. manipulated and pressured followers to embrace the vision
    c. shifted positions frequently to express contradictory values
    d. viewed mistakes as a normal part of doing things

13. Bennis and Nanus proposed that an appealing vision serves all but which one of the following functions?

   a. increase the leader's reward power
   b. facilitate initiative and discretion by followers
   c. give meaning to the work
   d. make followers feel important

14. Successful transformational leaders are least likely to:

   a. develop commitment among internal and external stakeholders
   b. embed new values and assumptions in the culture of the organization
   c. surround themselves with subordinates who are loyal and uncritical
   d. articulate an appealing vision of what the organization could become

15. Which of the following is least desirable for a vision?

   a. it should describe a desirable future in ideological terms
   b. it should be easy to understand
   c. it should be bold and ambitious
   d. it should include detailed action steps to make it credible

16. Which of the following was not recommended as a guideline for transformational leaders?

   a. continually emphasize the obstacles and dangers so followers will not become complacent about them
   b. recognize each person's contributions as the group strives to attain the vision
   c. use positive language that conveys optimism and confidence
   d. celebrate small successes to build the confidence of followers

17. Which of the following was not recommended as a guideline for transformational leaders?

   a. make followers feel responsible for failure of the old strategy to increase their commitment to the new one
   b. use dramatic, symbolic actions to emphasize key values in the vision
   c. use rites of transition to help people express their grief and anger about giving up sentimental aspects of the old culture
   d. lead by example to demonstrate in daily behavior the values espoused in the vision

18. Which of the following was not recommended as a guideline for leaders to strengthen the culture of an organization?

   a. centralize responsibility for cultural maintenance in top management
   b. identify core values and principles to preserve rather than specific practices
   c. use orientation programs, training programs, and special assignments to convey key values to new members of the organization
   d. emphasize key values in rituals, ceremonies, and rites of passage

Chapter 13: Strategic Leadership by Top Executives

1. Attributional research shows that most people:

   a. overestimate the effect leaders have on organizational performance
   b. underestimate the effect leaders have on organizational performance
   c. are able to accurately assess a leader's impact on organization performance
   d. are biased to look for weaknesses and faults in high level leaders

2. A leader is most likely to be viewed as effective when:

   a. organization performance is declining, the leader makes major changes in strategy, and performance rapidly improves
   b. organization performance is declining, the leader makes major changes in strategy, and performance slowly improves
   c. organization performance is declining, the leader makes small changes in strategy, and performance slowly improves
   d. organization performance is improving and the leader makes only incremental changes in the existing strategy to fine tune it

3. What is the best summary of the findings in research on effects of leadership succession?

   a. chief executives have little influence on organization performance due to the overwhelming influence of other factors such as economic and market conditions
   b. chief executives have a strong impact on organization performance and are the primary determinant of whether the organization prospers or declines
   c. chief executives have a moderate impact on organizational performance when measured over a period of several years
   d. chief executives influence stock prices but have little or no influence on the firm's actual economic performance

4. Which condition does not limit a chief executive's discretion to make major changes in the strategy of an organization?

   a. the organization has a few major clients who account for most sales
   b. the organization has surplus financial reserves
   c. the culture of the organization is strong
   d. the organization has a strong board of directors

5. A new chief executive is likely to have the most influence on organization performance when:

   a. the environment is stable and the organization is prosperous
   b. the environment is changing but the organization is still prosperous
   c. the environment is changing and organization performance is declining
   d. the environment is changing and performance has declined to the point where the organization is close to bankruptcy

6. The <u>least</u> likely response by a CEO faced with declining demand or new competition is to:

   a. improve implementation of the existing strategy (do more of the same)
   b. make small, incremental changes in the strategy
   c. discount the seriousness of the threat
   <u>d</u>. make major changes in the strategy

7. Research finds that most major reorientations in companies are initiated by:

   a. a strong chief executive who has occupied the position for many years
   b. an internal successor selected by the prior chief executive before retiring
   c. an internal successor selected to replace the prior CEO who was forced out
   <u>d</u>. an external successor brought in to replace the prior CEO who was forced out

8. According to Miller, what is most likely to happen over a period of several years if top management continues to refine and strengthen a narrow strategy that has been successful in the past?

   a. performance will slowly improve
   <u>b</u>. performance will improve at first, then begin to decline
   c. performance will decline at first, then begin to improve
   d. performance will rapidly improve

9. What pattern of behavior is most likely to occur with a chief executive who has been in office for three or four years?

   a. after the CEO consolidates power, he or she becomes more willing to experiment with innovative strategies
   b. as the CEO gains confidence with a strategy that is working, he or she becomes more excited about gathering information to evaluate and refine the strategy
   <u>c</u>. after the CEO selects a strategy and implements it, he or she becomes complacent and inflexible about changing it
   d. after the CEO institutionalizes power, he or she becomes more willing to allow others to participate in making major decisions

10. What pattern of behavior is <u>least</u> likely during the first few months on the job for the new CEO in an organization that is prosperous?

   <u>a</u>. the CEO will quickly select a new strategy and make major changes in the organization to look like a confident and dynamic leader
   b. the CEO will make changes in the functional areas in which he or she has the most prior experience
   c. the CEO will attempt to demonstrate some small successes in dealing with immediate problems in order to build a favorable image and gain more discretion
   d. the CEO will gather and analyze information about the organization and environment in order to determine an appropriate strategy

11. In what situation are executive teams <u>least</u> likely to be useful?

    a. the organization includes several business units with very diverse products
    <u>b</u>. there is intense competition among executives to become the successor of the current CEO
    c. the organization has a complex and turbulent environment
    d. the executives in the team have very diverse backgrounds and perspectives

12. Which of the following actions by the CEO is <u>least</u> likely to improve the effectiveness of an executive team?

    a. clearly define objectives that are consistent with shared values of team members
    <u>b</u>. resolve most issues by meeting individually with team members so that less time is needed for team meetings
    c. give the team considerable discretion but specify limits of team authority in relation to CEO authority
    d. help the team establish norms about group processes to facilitate working together effectively

13. Which procedure is <u>least</u> likely to improve the decisions made by executive teams?

    a. tactical action plans are considered before a final decision is made
    b. the CEO relies more on advice from members with the most expertise
    c. each decision is considered in relation to other strategic decisions rather than alone
    <u>d</u>. alternatives are examined sequentially rather than simultaneously

14. Which of the following was <u>not</u> described as an important future challenge for executives?

    <u>a</u>. the increasing popularity of large, bureaucratic organizations with vertical integration of operations
    b. the globalization of economies with more competition, multinational firms, and joint ventures
    c. the increasing diversity of the workforce due to different ethnic and cultural backgrounds
    d. the increasing technological complexity of products, processes, and information

15. Which of the following was <u>not</u> a recommended guideline for managing organizational transformation?

    a. select a top management team of executives who are committed to the vision
    b. develop a strategy for change with a few clear themes relevant to the shared values of organization members
    <u>c</u>. specify detailed guidelines on how to implement the strategy at all levels in the organization
    d. change the organization structure to be consistent with the new strategy

Chapter 14:   Leadership in Decision Making Groups

1. The primary responsibility of the leader of a decision group is to:

    a. suggest good ideas for solving the problem
    b. explain the reason for the problem
    c. encourage group members to reach an agreement quickly
    d. structure the discussion in a systematic manner

2. Which of the following is not a task-oriented function of group leaders?

    a. clarifying
    b. gatekeeping
    c. summarizing
    d. stimulating communication

3. Which of the following is not a group maintenance function of a group leader?

    a. consensus testing
    b. standard setting
    c. process analyzing
    d harmonizing

4. At the beginning of a meeting, it is most essential to:

    a. summarize progress made by the group in earlier meetings
    b. establish fairness as a standard
    c. clarify the purpose of the meeting
    d. have the group agree how it will arrive at a decision

5. A groupthink decision is least likely to be caused by:

    a. high group cohesiveness
    b. illusion of invulnerability
    c. legitimization of dissent
    d. illusion of morality

6. Which of the following is not a characteristic of groupthink?

    a. more effective decisions
    b. stereotyping of outgroups
    c. rationalization of unfavorable information
    d. self-censorship

7. What is the major advantage of a consensus decision as compared to a majority vote?

    a. it helps to reduce polarization
    b. the group is less biased by the leader's preferences
    c. it is more likely to result in a compromise
    d. group members are more committed to the decision

8. Which of the following is <u>least</u> likely to be a benefit of periodic summarizing by the leader during problem solving?

   a. getting the discussion back on course
   b. checking on understanding
   c. evaluating progress
   <u>d</u>. mediating conflict between members

9. Which of the following is <u>not</u> characteristic of Bradford's group-centered leadership?

   a. the leader should emphasize group maintenance behavior as much as task-oriented behavior
   b. the leader should encourage members to share the responsibility for performing leadership functions
   <u>c</u>. the leader should strive to maintain a rational discussion without emotional outbursts or expression of feelings
   d. the leader should allow the group to make the final choice

10. Which two procedures are used primarily for increasing idea generation by a group?

    a. brainstorming and delphi procedure
    <u>b</u>. brainstorming and nominal group technique
    c. nominal group technique and dialectical inquiry
    d. delphi procedure and dialectical inquiry

11. Which technique utilizes fantasy and analogy?

    <u>a</u>. synectics
    b. dialectical inquiry
    c. brainstorming
    d. solution integration

12. The nominal group technique:

    a. is always anonymous
    b. uses full discussion of ideas as the first step
    c. is the same as the delphi group technique
    <u>d</u>. seems to lead to more ideas than interacting groups

13. When a leader states a problem to the group, which of the following is <u>not</u> desirable according to Maier?

    a. the initial statement of the problem should be brief
    <u>b</u>. the problem should be stated in behavioral terms rather than in situational terms
    c. essential information should be shared with subordinates
    d. only one major objective should be stated

14. Which of the following is recommended by Maier for presenting a problem to the group?

 a. suggest possible reasons for the problem
 <u>b</u>. describe the problem in situational terms
 c. suggest a variety of objectives to consider in solving the problem
 d. interpret facts for the group whenever possible

15. Which of the following is <u>not</u> a recommended action for the leader during group problem solving discussions?

 <u>a</u>. encourage acceptance of the first feasible solution
 b. try to involve all members in the discussion
 c. ask exploratory but not judgmental questions
 d. delay the evaluation of solutions to prolong solution generation

16. Which of the following leader actions is <u>least</u> likely to improve the decision reached by a group?

 a. encourage positive restatement and idea building
 b. separate idea generation and evaluation
 c. equalize participation in evaluating ideas
 <u>d</u>. encourage polarization to sharpen debate

17. What procedure is <u>least</u> useful to avoid groupthink decisions?

 a. assign devil's advocates to critique the favorite solution
 b. ask each group member to list advantages and disadvantages for each solution
 <u>c</u>. encourage the group to continue meeting until they reach a consensus
 d. hold a second chance meeting to re-evaluate solutions

Chapter 15:   Overview and Integration

1. The trait studies of leadership effectiveness are most relevant to which approach for improving leadership?

 a. feedback workshops
 <u>b</u>. assessment and selection
 c. situational engineering
 d. training

2. The most widely used approach for improving leadership is:

 <u>a</u>. formal training programs
 b. assessment centers
 c. situational engineering
 d. action learning

3. What training method is most effective for learning interpersonal skills?

   a. management games and simulations
   b. behavior role modeling
   c. Leader Match
   d. case analysis in discussion groups

4. What was found in research to evaluate the effects of leadership training?

   a. there was no evidence of any significant improvement in leader effectiveness
   b. most of the training is highly effective, regardless of the training method
   c. some training methods are effective in improving some types of leadership skills
   d. training changes the attitudes of leaders but not their behavior back on the job

5. In most feedback workshops for management development, the main source of information about a manager's behavior is obtained from:

   a. other managers who participate in the workshop and fill out a checklist
   b. observers who record the person's behavior during a simulation
   c. watching a videotape taken of the manager at work
   d. questionnaires filled out by people with whom the manager works

6. Research at the Center for Creative Leadership suggests that _less_ learning occurred for managers who had:

   a. assignments for which they were well prepared
   b. challenges they had to face alone
   c. opportunities to make mistakes
   d. diverse experiences with different types of challenges

7. Selection and learning from experience are _____ approaches for improving leadership.

   a. mutually facilitating
   b. totally unrelated
   c. compatible
   d. somewhat incompatible

8. Which of the following statements about learning by top executives is _not_ accurate?

   a. feelings of confidence and superiority cause many executives to ignore or discount criticism and negative feedback
   b. top executives tend to become isolated from most people except other executives who are also isolated
   c. the realization that they have made it to the top causes executives to become less defensive and more open to feedback
   d. executives receive much praise but little criticism from people who are afraid of them or want to make a favorable impression

9. Which approach for improving leadership usually includes a mix of formal training and learning from experience working on management projects?

    a. mentoring
    b. feedback workshops
    c̲. action learning
    d. behavior modeling

10. An examination of trends in leadership research indicates all but which of the following?

    a. more research on cross-cultural differences in leadership
    b. more research on leadership as a shared process embedded within social systems
    c. more research using descriptive, qualitative data collection methods
    d̲. more research using longitudinal field experiments with multiple measures